E S T A T E   P U B L I C

COLCHESTER · CI

HARWICH · FRINTON · WALTON · BRIGHTLINGS
KELVEDON · MANNINGTREE · WEST MERSEA ·

C000160515

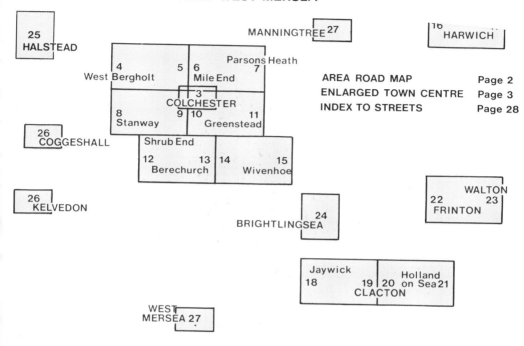

| 25 HALSTEAD |
| MANNINGTREE 27 |
| 16 HARWICH |

| 4 West Bergholt | 5 | 6 Mile End | 7 Parsons Heath |
| 3 COLCHESTER |
| 8 Stanway | 9 | 10 | 11 Greenstead |

AREA ROAD MAP   Page 2
ENLARGED TOWN CENTRE   Page 3
INDEX TO STREETS   Page 28

| 26 COGGESHALL |
| Shrub End |
| 12 | 13 Berechurch | 14 | 15 Wivenhoe |

| 26 KELVEDON |
| 24 BRIGHTLINGSEA |
| 22 FRINTON | 23 WALTON |

| Jaywick 18 | 19 | 20 CLACTON | Holland on Sea 21 |

| WEST MERSEA 27 |

Every effort has been made to verify the
accuracy of information in this book
but the publishers cannot accept
responsibility for expense or loss caused
by any error or omission. Information
that will be of assistance to the user of
the maps will be welcomed.

The representation of a road, track or
footpath on the maps in this atlas is no
evidence of the existence of a right of way.

One-way Street	→
Car Park	🅿
Place of Worship	+
Post Office	●
Public Convenience	⊙
Pedestrianized	▨

Scale of street plans 4 inches to 1 mile
Unless otherwise stated

Street plans prepared and published by ESTATE PUBLICATIONS, Bridewell House,
TENTERDEN, KENT, and based upon the ORDNANCE SURVEY mapping with the
permission of The Controller of H. M. Stationery Office.

The publishers acknowledge the co-operation of the local
authorities of towns represented in this atlas.

ROAD MAP

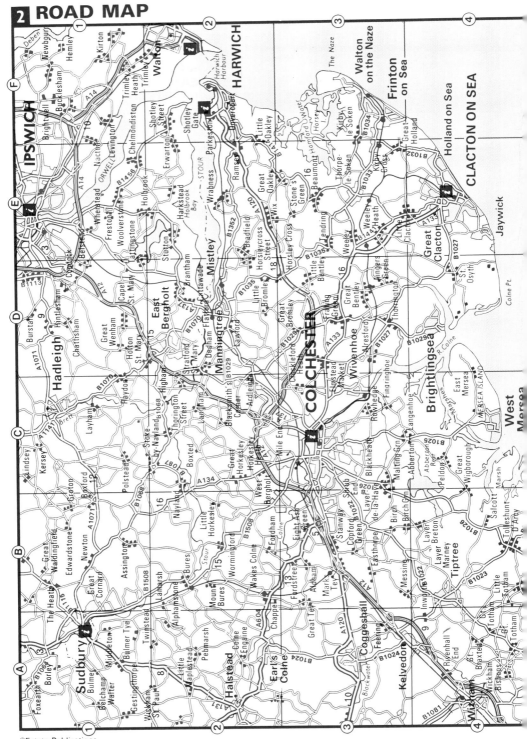

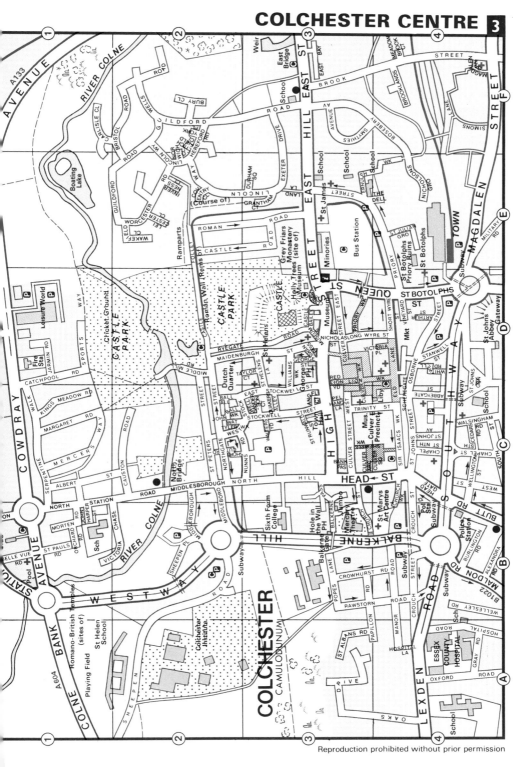

COLCHESTER
CAMULODUNUM

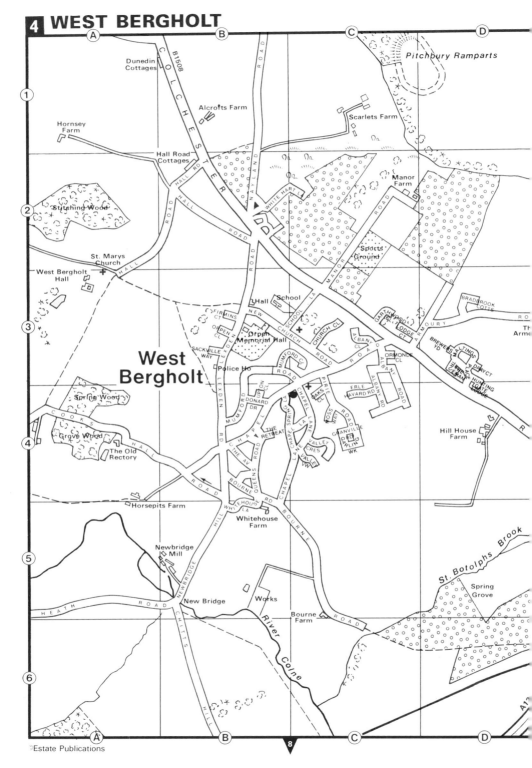

4 WEST BERGHOLT

Pitchbury Ramparts

Dunedin Cottages

Alcrofts Farm

Scarlets Farm

Hornsey Farm

Hall Road Cottages

Manor Farm

Stitching Wood

COLCHESTER ROAD B1508

NAYLAND ROAD

WHITE HART LA

St. Marys Church

West Bergholt Hall

HALL ROAD

Sports Ground

MANOR ROAD

BRADBROOK COTTS

School

Hall

FIRMINS CT

ORPEN CL

NEW CHURCH ROAD

SCHOOL LA

CHURCH CL

GARTHWOOD CL

LODGE

ARMOURY

The Armed

West Bergholt

Orpen Memorial Hall

SACKVILLE WAY

LEXDEN ROAD

MUMFORD RD

UNION CL

MUMFORD RD

CHURCH ROAD

ALBAN CL

ORMONDE CL

BREWERS SALTINGS

DEPOT

HUNTING

LODGE

Police Ho

DONARD DR

CHAPEL LA

PIRIE RD

OAKS WAY

ERLE HAVARD RD

ALBANY RD

ALBANY ROAD

Spring Wood

THE AV

THE RETREAT

CHAPEL LANE

ROSS WAY

CHAPEL LA

VALLEY CRES

GRANVILLE

GARLING WK

Hill House Farm

Grove Wood

COOKS HALL

The Old Rectory

CHAPEL HILL

QUEENS RD

BOURNE RD

VALLEY VW

Horsepits Farm

WH'HOUSE LA

Whitehouse Farm

BOURNE RD

St. Botolphs Brook

HEATH ROAD

Newbridge Mill

NEWBRIDGE HILL

CHITTS HILL

New Bridge

Works

Bourne Farm

Spring Grove

ROAD

River Colne

A12

8

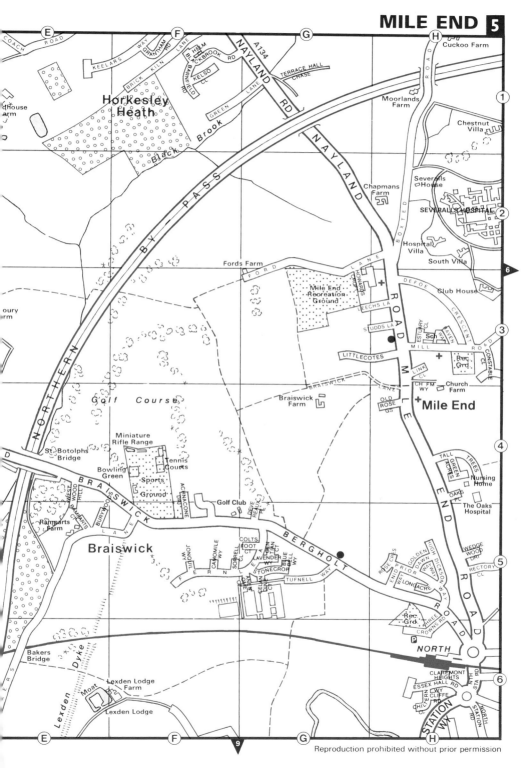

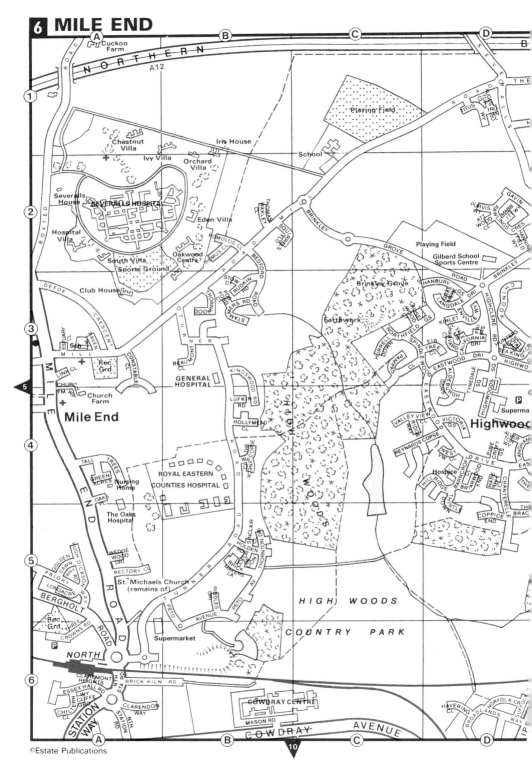

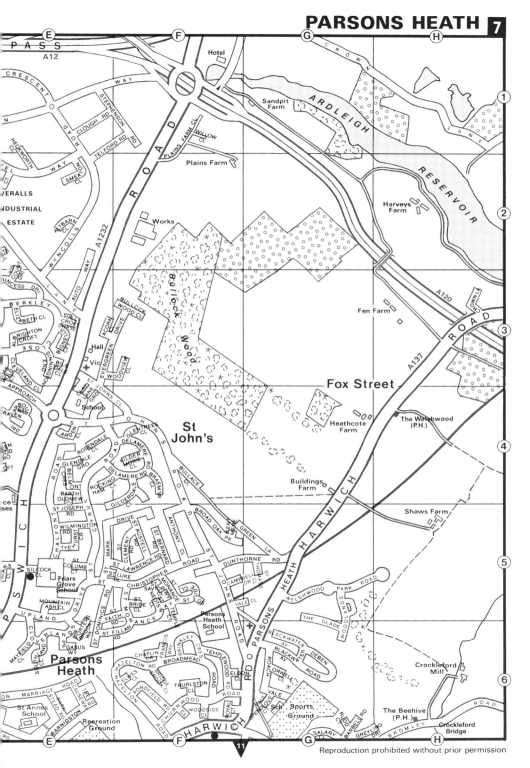

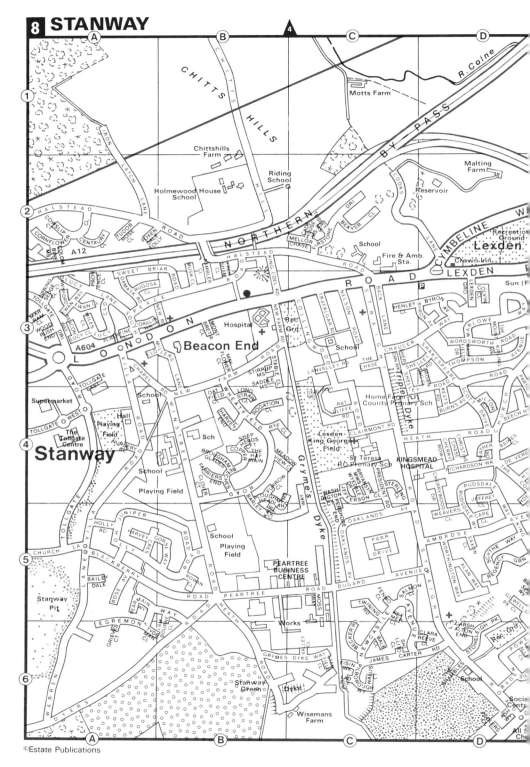

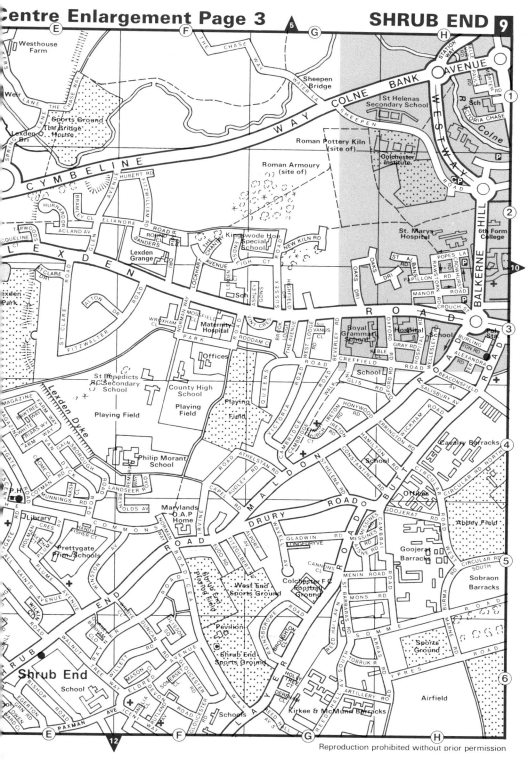

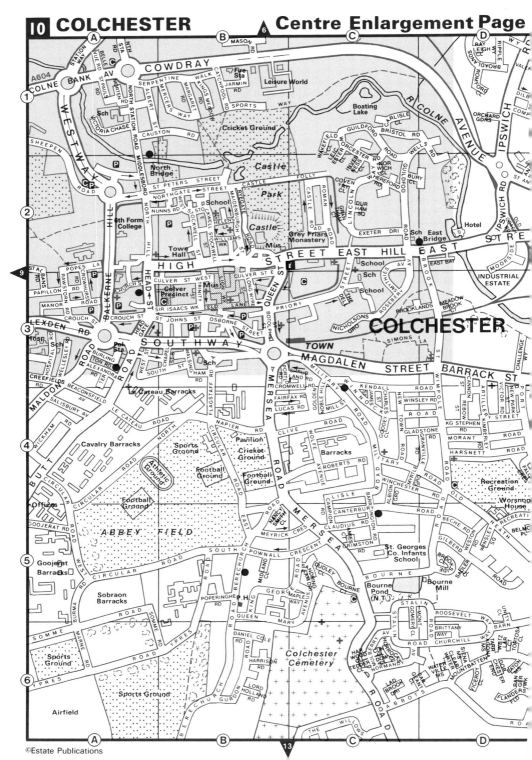

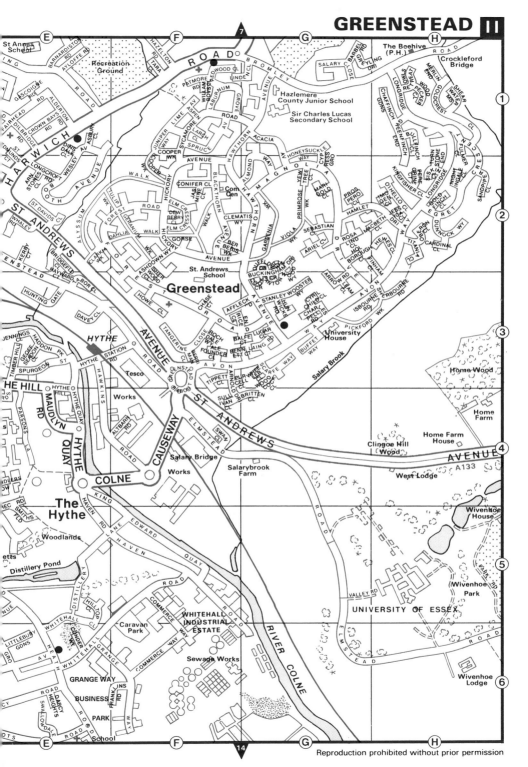

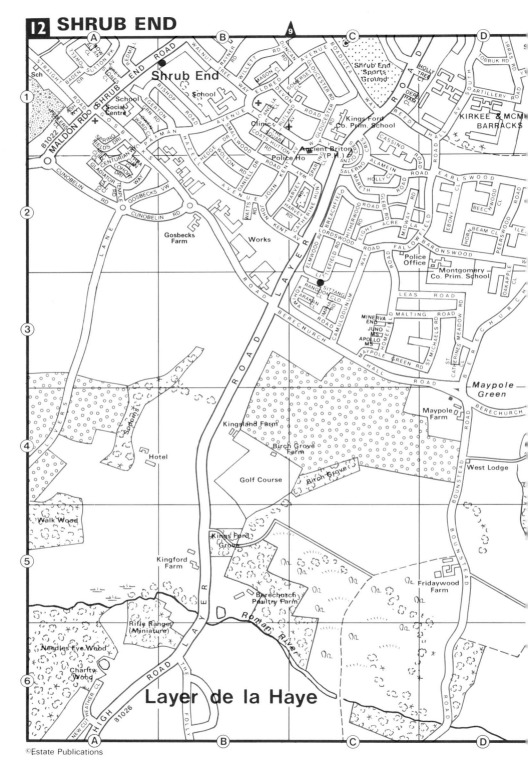

Shrub End

Layer de la Haye

KIRKEE & MCM BARRACKS

Maypole Green

Gosbecks Farm

Kingsland Farm

Birch Grove Farm

Golf Course

Walk Wood

Kingford Farm

Kings Ford Grove

Needles Eye Wood

Charity Wood

Rifle Range (Miniature)

Berechurch Poultry Farm

Fridaywood Farm

Maypole Farm

West Lodge

Shrub End Sports Ground

Kings Ford Co. Prim. School

Montgomery Co. Prim. School

Police Office

Ancient Briton (P.H.)

Police Ho

School

School

Social Centre

Clinic

Hotel

Works

Roman River

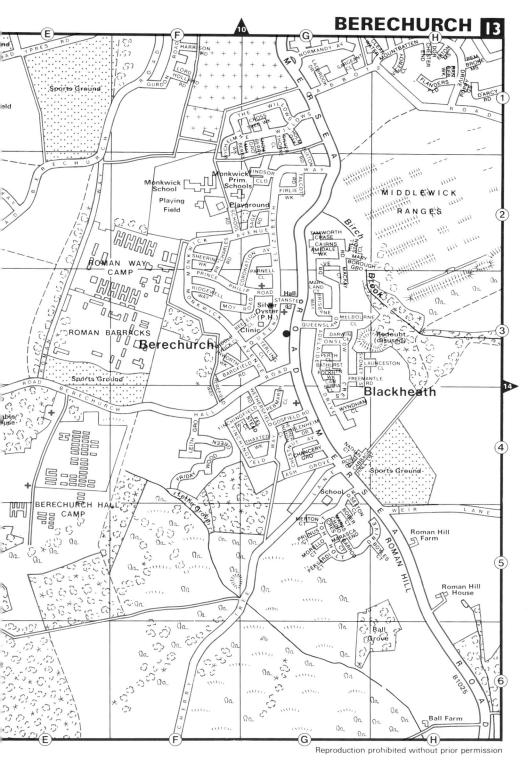

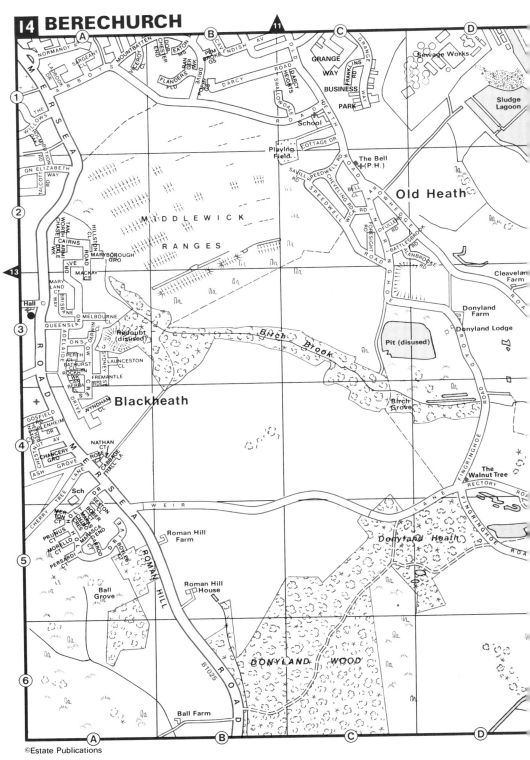

14 BERECHURCH

©Estate Publications

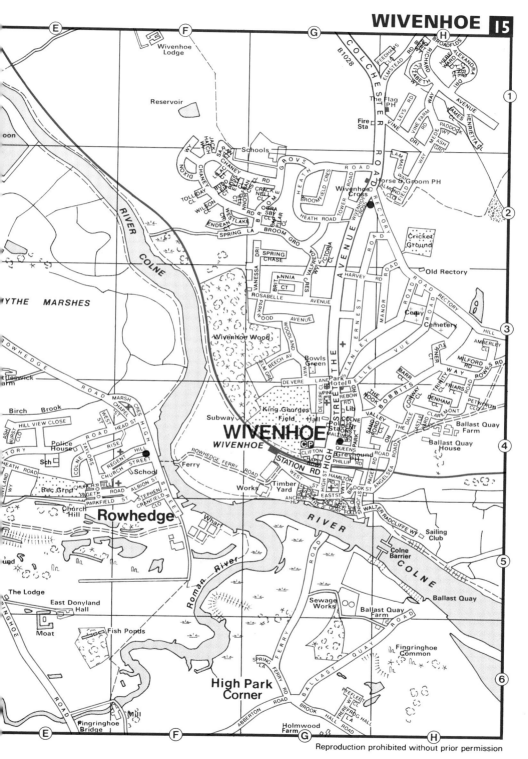

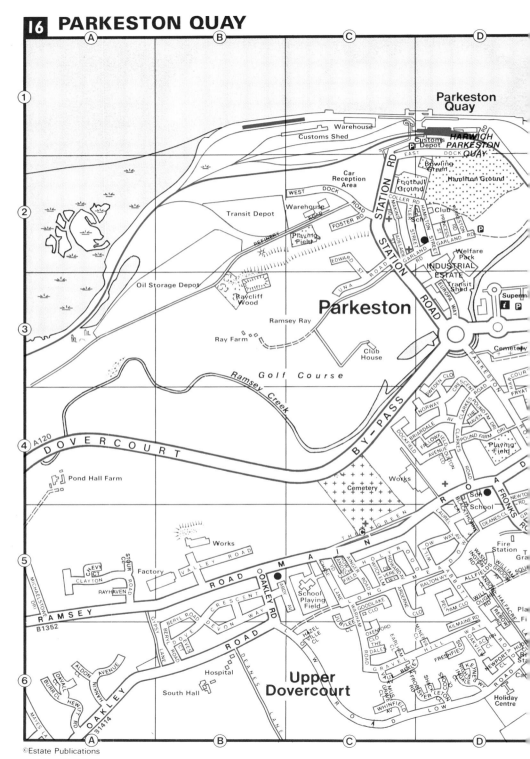

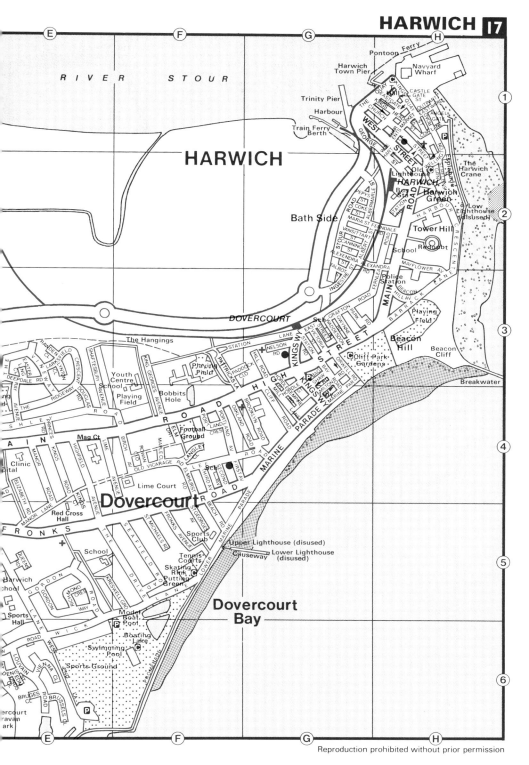

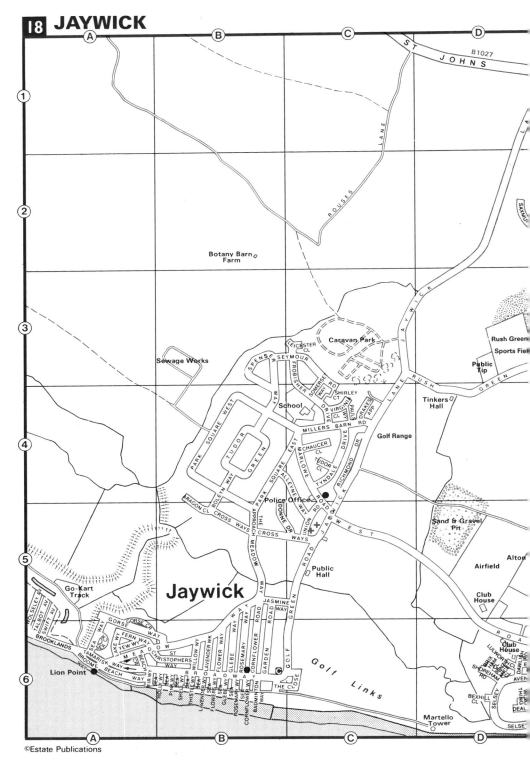

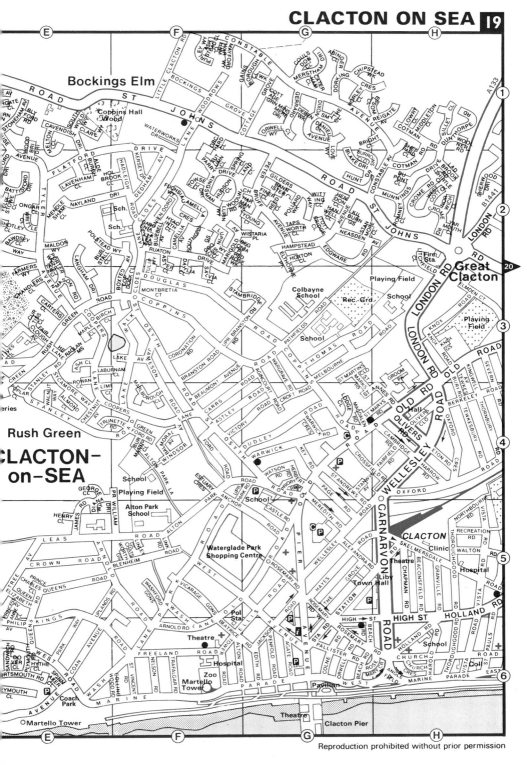

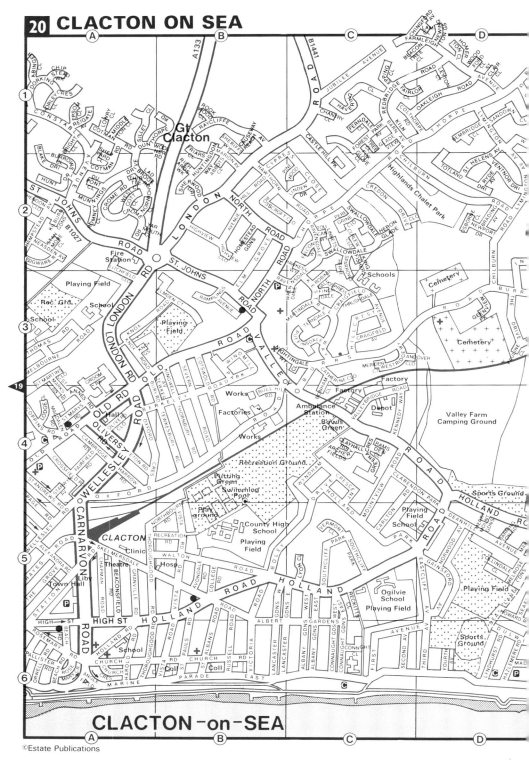

CLACTON -on-SEA

OAKWOOD BUSINESS PARK

Willow Farm

INDUSTRIAL ESTATE

STEPHENSON WAY

STEPHENSON ROAD WEST

PAXTON RD

SELDEN CT

BRINDLEY RD

BRUNEL

WADE RD

DAY RD

TELFORD ROAD

BURRS ROAD

INDUSTRIAL ESTATE

GORSE LANE CLOSE

KEITH

WILSON CT

Hall

HEATHER CL

GREENWAY

AVENUE

Burrsville Park

SLADBURYS

LANE

Great Holland Common

Holland Brook

DERWENT GDNS

DOVEDALE GDNS

LAKESWICK

Pickers   Ditch

B1032 ROAD

SLADE ROAD

BRENTWOOD ROAD

CHELMSFORD ROAD

COLCHESTER ROAD

WINDERMERE ROAD

HILLSIDE CRES

IPSWICH ROAD

STRATFORD ROAD

NANSEN ROAD

FLEETWOOD

MERRILEES CRES

FLEET CL

HUCKLES BURY AV

ELMNELL CL

SUFFOLK

PICKERS WAY

BEV WAY

BROADMERE CL

KENTS AV

NORFOLK

GRENFELL

OAKWOOD AV

P

FRINTON

PRESTON ROAD

PRINCES ROAD

KENILWORTH RD

NOTTINGHAM RD

MANCHESTER RD

HEREFORD RD

ROAD

PEMBROKE GDNS

SUSSEX GDNS

GRENFELL

PARK

BOULEVARD

BRIARWOOD

AYLESBURY DRIVE

Holland Bridge

Holland-on-Sea

☐ Hall

ROADS

ROAD

School

Rec. Grd.

HEREFORD

GARFIELD RD

EDISON RD

FRINTON

SAXON WAY

DULWICH ROAD

MADEIRA ROAD

QUEENSWAY

YORK

CANTERBURY

PRIMROSE ROAD

THE CHASE

FERNWOOD RD

BRIGHTON ROAD

BOURNEMOUTH RD

HALL CL

VIKING WAY

GEDDEL WAY

NEW DIN

STH HALL

SON DALE CL

HAVEN AV

MANOR WAY

Boat Compound

P

P

ISBURY

FORD

ROAD

NIX

CLIFF ROAD

KINGS PARADE

PARADE

THE ESPLANADE

THE GAP

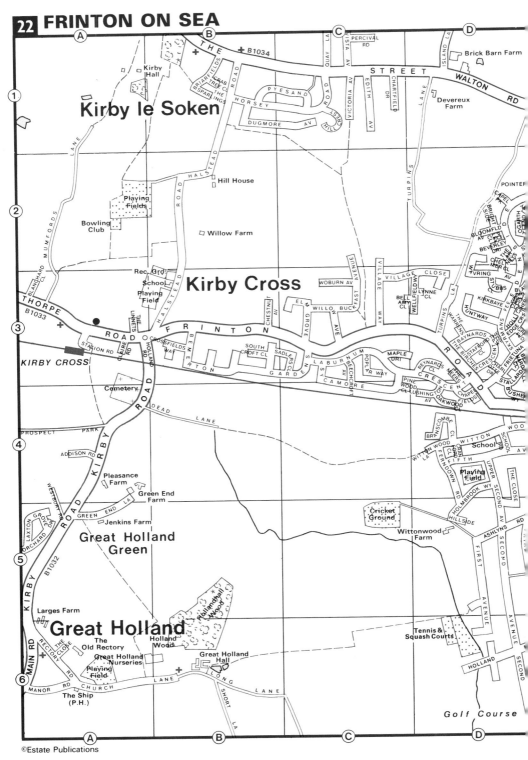

Kirby le Soken

Kirby Cross

Kirby Hall

Brick Barn Farm

Devereux Farm

Hill House

Playing Fields

Bowling Club

Willow Farm

Rec. Grd.

School

Playing Field

KIRBY CROSS

Cemetery

Prospect Park

Addison Rd

Pleasance Farm

Green End Farm

Jenkins Farm

Great Holland Green

Cricket Ground

Wittonwood Farm

Playing Field

School

Larges Farm

Great Holland

The Old Rectory

Great Holland Nurseries

Playing Field

Holland Wood

Hatfield Wood

Great Holland Hall

Tennis & Squash Courts

The Ship (P.H.)

Golf Course

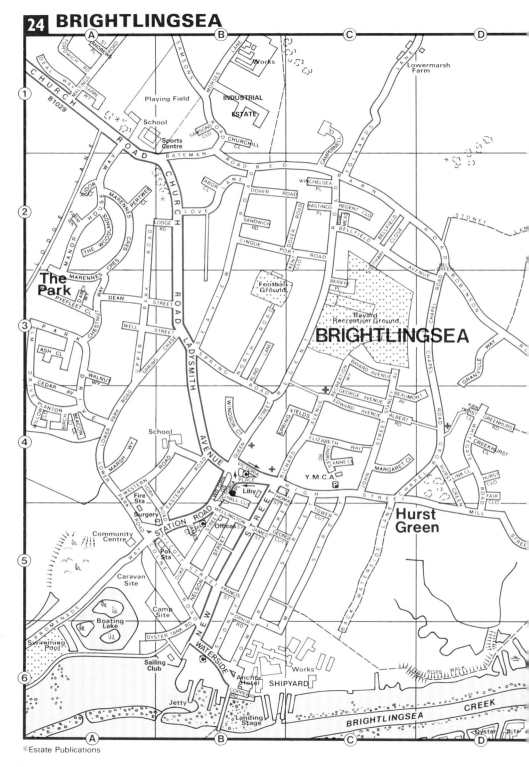

BRIGHTLINGSEA

The Park

Hurst Green

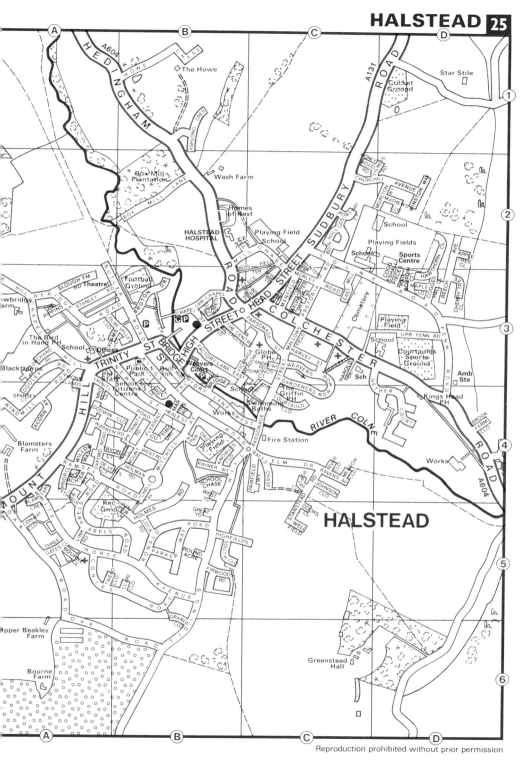

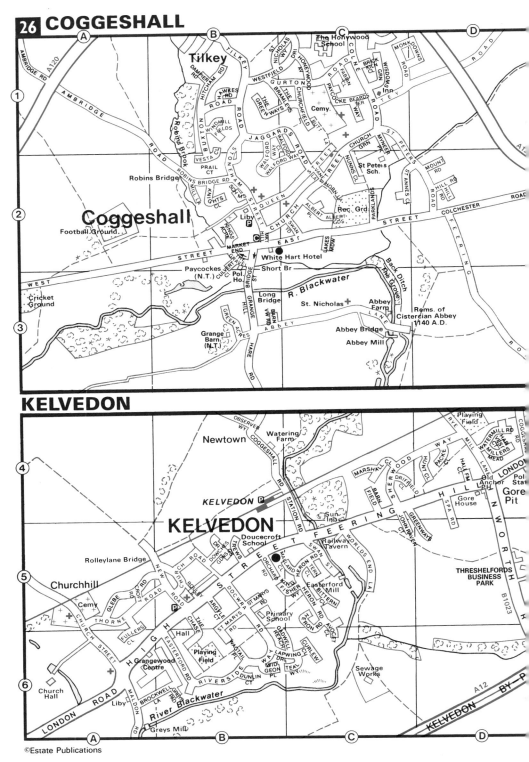

KELVEDON

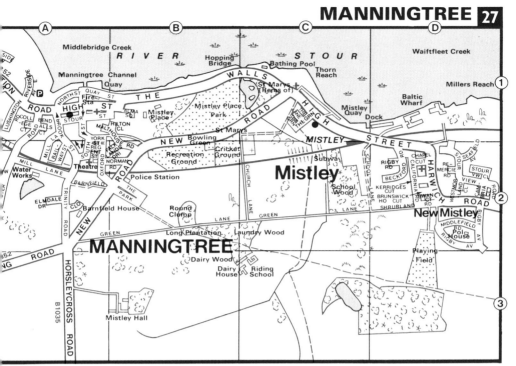

WEST MERSEA

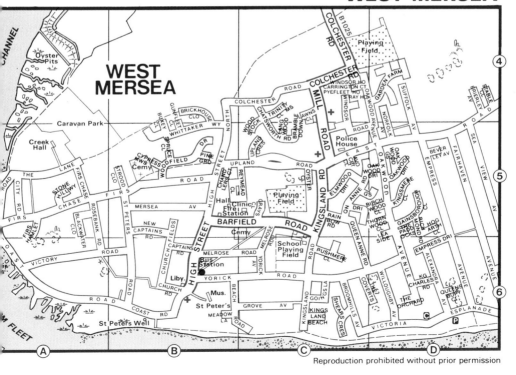

A - Z INDEX TO STREETS
with Postcodes

The Index includes some names for which there is insufficient space on the maps. These names are preceded by an * and are followed by the nearest adjoining thoroughfare.

28

Clacton area (cont.)	
The Lane. CO15	19 E3
Third Av. CO15	20 D6
Thirtle Clo. CO16	19 H2
Thomas Rd. CO15	19 G3
Thornbury Rd. CO15	19 H4
Thorndon Clo. CO16	19 E1
Thoroughgood Rd. CO15	19 H6
Thorpe Rd. CO15	20 C2
Thrushdale. CO15	20 C3
Totland Dri. CO15	20 D2
Totteridge Clo. CO16	19 G2
Toucan Way. CO15	20 C2
Tower Rd. CO15	19 F6
Towse Clo. CO15	19 F2
Trafalgar Rd. CO15	19 F6
Tree Clo. CO15	20 C1
Trunette Rd. CO15	19 F4
Tudor Clo. CO15	18 C4
Tudor Grn. CO15	18 B4
Tulip Way. CO16	19 F3
Turpins Av. CO15	20 D6
Turpins Clo. CO15	20 D5
Tyler Av. CO16	19 E2
Tyndale Dri. CO15	18 C4
Union Rd. CO15	18 C5
Uplands Rd. CO15	19 E5
Upper Branston Rd. CO15	19 F3
Upper Park Rd. CO15	19 F4
Valley Rd. CO15	20 B3
Valleybridge Rd. CO15	20 C4
Ventnor Dri. CO15	20 D2
Vermont Clo. CO15	20 C5
Vicarage Gdns. CO15	19 F5
Victoria Rd. CO15	20 B6
Victory Rd. CO16	19 F4
Viking Way. CO15	21 G6
Virginia Clo. CO15	18 C4
Vista Rd. CO15	19 H5
Wade Rd. CO15	21 E2
Walnut Way. CO15	19 E4
Walton Rd. CO15	19 H5
Wargrave Rd. CO15	19 G3
Warham Clo. CO16	19 F1
Warwick Cres. CO15	19 G4
Warwick Rd. CO15	19 G4
Wash La. CO15	19 F5
Washford Gdns. CO15	19 F5
Waterworks Dri. CO16	19 F1
Watson Rd. CO15	19 G4
Wellesley Rd. CO15	19 H4
West Av. CO15	19 F5
West Rd. CO15	18 C5
Westcott Clo. CO16	19 H2
Westridge Way. CO15	20 C3
Weymouth Clo. CO15	19 E6
Willow Way. CO15	18 B6
Wilson Ct. CO15	21 E2
Windermere Rd. CO15	21 E5
Windmill Pk. CO15	20 B3
Windsor Av. CO15	19 F4
Wistaria Pl. CO16	19 G2
Witting Rd. CO15	19 G2
Wolseley Av. CO15	18 A5
Woodbridge Rd. CO16	19 E1
Woodford Clo. CO15	20 D1
Woodlands Clo. CO15	20 D1
Woodrows. CO16	19 F1
Woolner Rd. CO16	19 H1
Woolwich Rd. CO16	19 F2
Worthing Mews. CO15	18 D6
Wrendale. CO15	20 C3
Writtle Clo. CO15	19 E2
Wyndham Cres. CO15	20 C4
Yarmouth Clo. CO16	19 H2
Yew Way. CO15	18 A6
York Rd. CO15	21 F6
Young Clo. CO16	19 G2

COGGESHALL

Abbey La. CO6	26 B3
Albert Gdns. CO6	26 C2
Albert Pl. CO6	26 C2
Ambridge Rd. CO6	26 A1
Barn View Rd. CO6	26 B3
Beards Ter. CO6	26 C1
Brick Kiln Clo. CO6	26 C1
Bridge St. CO6	26 B3
Butt La. CO6	26 C1
Buxton Rd. CO6	26 B1
Church Grn. CO6	26 C1
Church St. CO6	26 B2
Churchfield. CO6	26 C1
Colchester Rd. CO6	26 D2
Colne Rd. CO6	26 B2
Culvert Clo. CO6	26 B2
Dampier Rd. CO6	26 B1
East St. CO6	26 B2
Fabian Clo. CO6	26 C1
Feering Rd. CO6	26 D2
Grange Hill. CO6	26 B3
Green Acres. CO6	26 B3
Gurton Rd. CO6	26 B1
Hare Rd. CO6	26 B3
Hawkes Rd. CO6	26 B1
Hill Rd. CO6	26 D2
Hitcham Rd. CO6	26 B1
Honeywood Av. CO6	26 C1
Horn La. CO6	26 C2
Jaggards Rd. CO6	26 B1
Kings Acre. CO6	26 B2
Knights Rd. CO6	26 B2
Lake Meadow. CO6	26 C2
Market End. CO6	26 B2
Market Hill. CO6	26 B2
Mill La. CO6	26 B2
Monkdowns Rd. CO6	26 C1
Mount Rd. CO6	26 D2
Myneer Pk. CO6	26 C1
Nunns Clo. CO6	26 C2
Parklands. CO6	26 C2
Paycocke Way. CO6	26 C1
Prail Ct. CO6	26 B2
Queen St. CO6	26 B2
Robins Bridge Rd. CO6	26 B2
St Annes Clo. CO6	26 C2
St Nichólas Way. CO6	26 B1
St Peters Rd. CO6	26 C1
School Mews. CO6	26 B2
Stoneham St. CO6	26 B2
Swan Yd. CO6	26 C2
Tey Rd. CO6	26 C1
The Bramleys. CO6	26 C1
The Gravel. CO6	26 B2
The Greenways. CO6	26 B1
Tilkey Rd. CO6	26 B1
Vane La. CO6	26 C2
Vesta Clo. CO6	26 B2
Walford Clo. CO6	26 C1
Walford Way. CO6	26 B2
West St. CO6	26 A3
Westfield Dri. CO6	26 B1
Windmill Fields. CO6	26 B1
Wisdoms Grn. CO6	26 C1

COLCHESTER

Abberton Rd. CO5	15 G6
Abbeygate St. CO2	3 C4
Abbots Rd. CO2	10 C6
Acacia Av. CO4	11 G1
Achnacone Dri. CO4	5 F4
Acland Rd. CO2	9 E2
Acorn Clo. CO4	7 E3
Adelaide Dri CO2	13 G3
Affleck Rd. CO4	11 F3
Aisne Rd. CO2	9 G5
Alamein Rd. CO2	12 C2
Alan Way. CO3	8 D5
Alanbrooke Rd. CO2	14 C2
Albany Clo. CO6	4 C3
Albany Rd. CO6	4 C3
Albert St. CO1	3 C1
Albertine Clo. CO3	8 A3
Albion Gro. CO2	10 C4
Albion St. CO5	15 F4
Albrighton Croft. CO4	7 E3
Aldeburgh Gdns. CO4	6 D3
Alderton Rd. CO4	11 E1
Alefounder Clo. CO4	11 F3
Alexandra Dri. CO7	15 H1
Alexandra Rd. CO3	3 B4
Alexandra Ter. CO3	10 A3
All Saints Av. CO3	9 E5
Alma St. CO7	15 G4
Almond Clo. CO5	15 H2
Almond Way. CO4	11 G2
Alport Av. CO2	9 G5
Altbarn Rd. CO2	11 F4
Altbarn Clo. CO4	7 E2
Alton Dri. CO3	9 E3
Alverton Way. CO4	6 D4
Alyssum Walk. CO4	11 E2
Amberley Clo. CO7	15 H3
Ambrose Av. CO3	8 D5
Amies Ct. CO2	10 C5
Anchor Hill. CO7	15 G4
Anemone Ct. CO4	5 G5
Angel Ct. CO2	3 C3
Angelsea Rd. CO7	15 H4
Anglia Clo. CO2	9 F6
Anthony Clo. CO4	7 F5
Anzio Cres. CO2	12 C2
Apollo Mews. CO2	12 C3
Arakan Clo. CO2	12 C3
Arbour Way. CO4	7 E4
Arden Clo. CO4	7 E4
Ariel Clo. CO4	11 G2
Armidale Walk. CO2	13 G2
Armoury Rd. CO6	4 C3
Arnold Dri. CO4	11 F3
Arnstones Clo. CO4	11 E2
Arras Rd. CO2	9 H6
Arrow Rd. CO4	11 G3
Arthur St. CO2	3 D4
Artillery Rd. CO2	9 G6
Artillery St. CO1	10 D4
Asbury Clo. CO4	11 E1
Ash Gro. CO2	13 G4
Ash Gro. CO7	15 H1
Ash Way. CO3	8 D6
Ashdown Way. CO4	11 F2
Ashhurst Clo. CO5	15 E4
Ashley Gdns. CO3	9 G3
Aspen Rd. CO4	11 F1
Athelstan Rd. CO3	9 G4
Attwood Clo. CO4	6 D2
Audley Rd. CO3	9 F4
Augustus Clo. CO4	6 D1
Auto Way. CO4	7 E3
Avignon Clo. CO2	10 D6
Avon Way. CO4	11 F3
Ayloffe Rd. CO4	11 E1
Back La. CO3	8 C3
Baden Powell Dri. CO3	8 D6
Bailey Dale. CO3	8 A5
Baines Clo. CO3	8 D4
Bakers La. CO4	9 E1
Bale Clo. CO3	8 C6
Balfe Ct. CO4	11 F3
Balkerne Hill. CO3	3 B4
Balkerne Pass. CO1	3 B3
Ball Alley. CO1	3 C2
Ball Walk. CO1	3 C2
Ballast Quay Rd. CO5	15 G6
Bank Pass. CO1	3 C3
Barbel Rd. CO4	7 G6
Bardfield Rd. CO2	13 F3
Barkstead Rd. CO4	7 E6
Barley Way. CO3	8 B4
Barn Hall Av. CO2	10 D6
Barnardiston Rd. CO4	11 E1
Barncroft Clo. CO4	6 D4
Barnfield Rd. CO6	5 F1
Baronia Croft. CO4	7 E4
Baronswood Way. CO2	12 D2
Barr Clo. CO7	15 H3
Barrack St. CO1	10 D3
Barrington Rd. CO5	10 C5
Bartholomew Clo. CO4	7 E4
Bath St. CO7	15 G4
Bathurst Clo. CO2	13 G3
Battlesbrook Rd. CO2	14 C2
Bawtree Way. CO3	9 E4
Beacon Way. CO3	8 A3
Beaconsfield Av. CO3	10 A4
Beaumont Clo. CO4	6 B3
Beaver Clo. CO3	8 C2
Beche Rd. CO2	10 D5
Becker Rd. CO3	8 C6
Bedford Rd. CO4	6 B2
Beech Av. CO7	15 G3
Beech Hill. CO3	8 D4
Beechwood Clo. CO2	12 D2
Beeleigh Clo. CO2	13 F3
Bell Clo. CO2	14 C2
Belle Vue Rd. CO1	3 B1
Belle Vue Rd. CO7	15 G3
Belmont Cres. CO4	7 E4
Belmont Pl. CO1	10 D
Bennett Ct. CO4	11
Berberis Walk. CO4	11
Berechurch Hall Rd. CO2	12
Berechurch Rd. CO2	10
Berefield Way. CO2	13
Bergholt Rd. CO4	5 C
Berkley Clo. CO4	7
Berriman Clo. CO4	11
Bethany St. CO5	15 C
Beverley Rd. CO3	9 C
Bignells Croft. CO4	7
Bilsdale Clo. CO4	7
Bishop Rd. CO2	9
Blackberry Rd. CO3	8
Blackbrook Rd. CO6	5
Blackthorn Av. CO4	11
Blackwater Av. CO4	7
Blenheim Dri. CO2	13
Bluebell Way. CO4	5
Boadicea Way. CO2	9
Bobbits Way. CO7	15
Bober Ct. CO2	13
Booth Av. CO4	11
Bounstead Rd. CO2	12
Bourne Clo. CO2	10
Bourne Rd. CO2	10
Bourne Rd. CO6	4
Bowes Rd. CO7	15
Boxted Rd. CO4	5
Boyles Ct. CO2	13
Bradbrook Cotts. CO6	4
Braemar Clo. CO4	7
Braiswick. CO4	5
Braiswick La. CO4	5
Bramley Clo. CO3	9
Breachfield Rd. CO2	12
Bream Ct. CO4	7
Brewers Yd. CO6	4
Briarwood End. CO4	6
Brick Kiln La. CO6	5
Brick Kiln Rd. CO7	6
Brickmakers La. CO4	6
Bridgebrook Clo. CO4	7
Bridgefield Clo. CO4	11
Brinkley Cres. CO4	7
Brinkley Gro Rd. CO4	6
Brinkley La. CO4	6
Brisbane Way. CO2	13
Bristol Rd. CO1	3
Brittania Court. CO7	15
Brittania Cres. CO7	15
Brittany Way. CO2	10
Britten Clo. CO4	11
Broad Oak Pk. CO4	7
Broadfields. CO7	15
Broadlands Way. CO4	6
Broadmead Rd. CO4	7
Bromley Rd. CO4	11
Brook Hall Rd. CO5	15
Brooklands. CO1	3
Brook Lodge. CO3	9
Brook St. CO1	3
Brookside Clo. CO2	10
Broome Gro. CO7	15
Broomfield Cres. CO7	15
Brougham Glades. CO3	8
Broughton Clo. CO2	9
Browning Clo. CO3	8
Brownsea Way. CO3	8
Brunel Ct. CO4	7
Brunel Way. CO4	7
Bryanston Mews. CO3	8
Buckingham Dri. CO4	11
Buddlea Ct. CO7	15
Buffet Way. CO4	11
Bullace Clo. CO4	7
Bullfinch Clo. CO4	11
Bullock Wood Clo. CO4	7
Burlington Rd. CO3	7
Burma Rd. CO2	9
Burns Av. CO3	8
Bury Clo. CO1	3
Burywoods. CO4	5
Butt Rd. CO3	3
Buxton Rd. CO2	13
Byron Av. CO3	8
Cabbage Hall La. CO2	14
Cadenhouse Mews. CO3	13
Cairns Rd. CO2	13

California Dri. CO4	6 D3
Cambrai Rd. CO2	9 H5
Cambridge Rd. CO3	9 G4
Cambridge Walk. CO3	9 G4
Camomile Way. CO4	5 F5
Campbell Dri. CO4	7 F5
Campion Rd. CO2	10 C5
Camulodunum Way. CO2	12 C3
Canberra Clo. CO2	13 G3
Cannon St. CO1	10 D3
Cannons Clo. CO2	9 G5
Canterbury Rd. CO2	10 C5
Canwick Gro. CO2	11 E6
Cape Clo. CO3	8 D5
Capel Rd. CO3	9 F4
Cappilar Clo. CO7	15 G2
Cardinal Clo. CO4	11 H2
Carlisle Clo. CO4	3 F1
Carlton Ct. CO5	15 E4
Caroline Clo. CO3	15 H1
Carshalton End. CO3	8 D6
Cassino Rd. CO2	12 C1
Castle Bailey. CO1	3 D3
Castle Folley. CO1	3 D2
Castle Rd. CO1	3 E2
Castle Ward Clo. CO7	15 H4
Catchpool Rd. CO1	3 D1
Catherine Hunt Way. CO2	12 C2
Causton Rd. CO1	3 C2
Cavendish Av. CO2	10 D6
Cedars Rd. CO2	3 C4
Celandine Ct. CO4	5 G5
Centaury Clo. CO3	8 A2
Centurion Way. CO2	12 A2
Chaffinch Gdns. CO4	11 H1
Chalfont Rd. CO4	7 E5
Challenge Way. CO1	10 D3
Chancery Gro. CO2	13 G4
Chandlers Row. CO1	11 E4
Chaney Rd. CO7	15 F2
Chanterelle. CO4	6 D4
Chapel La. CO6	4 C4
Chapel Rd. CO3	8 A3
Chapel Rd. CO6	4 B4
Chapel Row. CO7	15 G4
Chapel St. CO5	15 F4
Chapel St Nth. CO2	3 C4
Chapel St Sth. CO2	3 C4
Chaplin Dri. CO4	7 F6
Charles Pell Rd. CO4	11 G3
Charles St. CO1	10 C4
Chase Ct. CO4	11 F3
Chaucer Way. CO3	8 C3
Cherry Row. CO3	8 D4
Cherry Tree La. CO2	13 F6
Cherrywood Dri. CO3	8 D4
Chestnut Av. CO2	13 G4
Cheveling Rd. CO2	14 C2
Chiltern Clo. CO1	6 A6
Chinook. CO4	6 D3
Chitts Hill. CO3	8 B1
Christchurch Ct. CO3	9 G4
Christine Chase. CO3	8 D4
Church Clo. CO6	4 C3
Church Farm Way. CO4	6 A3
Church Hill. CO5	15 E4
Church La, Lexden. CO3	8 D4
Church La, Stanway. CO3	8 A5
Church St. CO1	3 B3
Church St. CO5	15 F4
Church Walk. CO1	3 C4
Churchill Way. CO2	10 D6
Churnwood Clo. CO4	7 F6
Churnwood Rd. CO4	7 F6
Circular Rd East. CO2	10 B4
Circular Rd Nth. CO2	10 A4
Circular Rd Sth. CO2	10 A5
Circular Rd West. CO2	10 A4
Clairmont Rd. CO3	8 C4
Clara Reeve Clo. CO3	8 D5
Claremont Heights. CO1	6 A6
Claremont Rd. CO7	15 H4
Clarendon Way. CO1	6 A6
Clarkia Walk. CO4	11 E2
Claudius Rd. CO2	10 C5
Claylane Gro. CO4	7 E4
Clearwater. CO2	10 D6
Clematis Way. CO4	11 F2
Cleveland Clo. CO4	7 E3
Clifton Ter. CO7	15 G4
Clive Rd. CO2	10 B4
Clough Rd. CO4	7 E1
Clover Ct. CO3	8 B4
Cloverlands. CO4	7 E5
Coach Rd. CO7	5 E1
Coats Hutton Rd. CO2	12 B1
Coeur de Lion. CO4	6 B5
Cohort St. CO2	12 A2
Colchester By-Pass. CO1	3 D1
Colchester Rd. CO6	4 B1
Colchester Rd. CO7	15 G1
Collingwood Rd. CO3	8 C3
Colne Bank Av. CO1	3 A1
Colne Causeway. CO4	15 E4
Colne Rise. CO5	15 E4
Colne Ter. CO7	15 G4
Colombine Mews. CO3	8 A2
Coltsfoot Ct. CO4	5 G5
Colvin Clo. CO3	8 D3
Commerce Way. CO1	11 F6
Compton Rd. CO4	10 D1
Conder Way. CO1	11 E6
Conifer Clo. CO4	11 F2
Constable Clo. CO4	6 A3
Constantine Rd. CO3	9 G4
Conway Clo. CO7	15 H3
Cook Cres. CO4	11 G3
Cooks Hall Rd. CO6	4 A4
Cooks La. CO3	8 C2
Cooper Walk. CO4	11 F1
Copper Beeches. CO3	8 B4
Coppice End. CO4	6 D5
Coralin Walk. CO3	8 A3
*Coriolanus Clo, Centurion Way. CO2	12 A2
Cornflower Clo. CO3	8 A2
Coronation Av. CO2	13 F3
Cotman Rd. CO3	9 E4
Cotswold Ct. CO4	7 E3
Cottage Dri. CO2	14 C1
Cotton Wood Clo. CO2	12 D2
Coventry Clo. CO1	3 E2
Cowdray Av. CO1	3 C1
Cowdray Clo. CO1	3 D2
Cowslip Ct. CO3	8 A2
Cracknell Clo. CO7	15 G2
Craven Dri. CO4	7 E4
Creefield Rd. CO3	10 A3
Crome Clo. CO3	9 E4
Cromwell Rd. CO2	10 B3
Crosstree Walk. CO3	13 G1
Crouch St. CO3	3 B4
Crowhurst Rd. CO3	3 B3
Crown Bays Rd. CO4	11 E1
Crown La. CO4	7 G1
Crown La. CO4	7 H3
Culver Arcade. CO1	3 C3
Culver Sq. CO1	3 C4
Culver St E. CO1	3 D3
Culver St W. CO1	3 C3
Culver Walk. CO1	3 C3
Cunobelin Rd. CO2	12 A2
Cunningham Clo. CO2	10 C6
Cymbeline Way. CO3	8 D2
Cypress Gro. CO4	11 G2
Cyril Child Clo. CO4	11 G3
D'Arcy Heights. CO2	11 E6
D'Arcy Rd. CO2	11 E6
Dahlia Walk. CO4	11 F2
Damask Rd. CO3	8 A3
Daniel Cole Rd. CO2	10 B6
Daniell Dri. CO2	12 B2
Darwin Clo. CO2	13 G3
Davey Clo. CO1	11 E3
Dawnford Clo. CO3	8 A3
De Vere Clo. CO7	15 G4
De Vere Rd. CO7	15 G3
De Vere Rd. CO4	8 D4
Deben Rd. CO4	7 G6
Deburgh Rd. CO3	8 C4
Defoe Cres. CO4	5 H3
Delamare Rd. CO4	7 E4
Denham Clo. CO7	15 H4
Dentons Ter. CO7	15 G4
Dereham Clo. CO2	12 C1
Derwent Rd. CO4	7 E3
Devereaux Pl. CO4	5 G5
Devon Rd. CO4	9 F6
Dewberry Clo. CO4	11 F2
Dilbridge Rd. CO4	10 D1
Dinsdale Clo. CO4	11 E1
Distillery La. CO2	11 E5
Dixon Way. CO7	15 F2
Donard Dri. CO6	4 B4
Donyland Way. CO5	15 E4
Dorchester End. CO2	10 D6
Dowding Clo. CO2	10 C6
Dray Ct. CO6	4 D3
Drury Rd. CO2	9 G5
Dudley Clo. CO2	10 C5
Duffield Dri. CO4	11 G2
Dugard Av. CO3	8 C5
Duncan Rd. CO2	9 F6
Dunnock Way. CO4	11 H2
Dunthorne Rd. CO4	7 F5
Durham Sq. CO1	3 E3
Dyers Rd. CO3	8 A6
Earlswood Way. CO2	12 D2
East Bay. CO1	3 F3
East Hill. CO1	3 E3
East Stockwell St. CO1	3 C3
East St. CO1	3 F3
East St. CO7	15 G4
Estuary Clo. CO4	6 A3
Eastwood Dri. CO4	6 D3
Eaton Mews. CO2	10 D6
Ebony Clo. CO2	12 D2
Edison Gdns. CO4	11 E1
Egerton Green Rd. CO2	9 E6
Egremont Way. CO3	8 A6
Egret Cres. CO4	11 H2
Eight Acre La. CO2	12 C2
Eld La. CO1	3 C4
Eldon Clo. CO4	7 F6
Eldred Av. CO2	9 F6
Elianore Rd. CO3	9 E2
Elizabeth Way. CO7	15 H1
Elm Cres. CO4	11 F2
Elm Gro. CO7	15 G3
Elmstead Rd. CO4	11 F4
Elmstead Rd. CO7	15 H1
Elmwood Av. CO2	12 C2
Elwes Clo. CO4	7 F6
Endean Ct. CO7	15 F2
Endsleigh Ct. CO3	9 F2
Enid Way. CO4	5 H5
Enville Way. CO4	6 D3
Erle Havard Rd. CO6	4 C4
Ernest Rd. CO7	15 G3
Ernulph Walk. CO1	3 E3
Errington Rd. CO3	9 H4
Essex Hall Rd. CO1	6 A6
Eudo Rd. CO2	9 F5
Evergreen Dri. CO4	7 E3
Ewan Clo. CO3	8 A3
Ewan Way. CO3	8 A3
Exeter Dri. CO1	3 E3
Fairfax Rd. CO2	10 B4
Fairfield Gdns. CO4	11 E2
Fairhead Rd. CO4	11 E1
Falcon Cres. CO1	10 D4
Fallowfield Rd. CO2	12 C2
Farriers End. CO3	8 B4
Feedhams Clo. CO7	15 H1
Felstead Clo. CO2	13 G4
Fenno Clo. CO3	8 C5
Fernlea. CO4	5 F5
Ferry Rd. CO5	15 G6
Field Way. CO7	15 H2
Finchingfield Way. CO4	13 F4
Fingringhoe Rd. CO2	14 C2
Finham St. CO4S	11 H2
Fir Tree Clo. CO4	6 D3
Firlie Walk. CO2	13 G2
Firmins Ct. CO6	4 B3
Firstore Dri. CO3	8 C2
Fisin Walk. CO3	8 C6
Fitzgilbert Rd. CO2	9 F5
Fitzwalter Rd. CO3	9 E3
Fitzwilliam Rd. CO3	9 F2
Flagstaff Rd. CO2	10 B4
Flanders Field. CO2	10 D6
Ford La. CO4	5 G3
Foresight Rd. CO2	14 C2
Forest Rd. CO4	11 F2
Foxendale Folly. CO3	8 A2
Francis Clo. CO7	15 G2
Francis Way. CO4	7 F6
Frank Clater Clo. CO4	10 D1
Franklins Rd. CO1	11 F6
Freemantle Rd. CO2	13 G3
Frensham Clo. CO3	8 B2
Frere Way. CO5	15 G6
Friars Clo. CO4	7 E5
Friars Clo. CO7	15 H3
Friday Wood Grn. CO2	13 F4
Frog Hall La. CO5	15 G6
Fullers Rd. CO4	14 C2
Fulmer Clo. CO4	11 H1
Furrow Clo. CO3	8 B4
Gainsborough Rd. CO3	9 E4
Gardenia Walk. CO4	11 G2
Garling Walk. CO6	4 C4
Garrod Ct. CO2	13 G5
Garthwood Clo. CO6	4 C3
Gascoigne Rd. CO4	11 E1
Gavin Way. CO4	6 D2
Gazelle Ct. CO4	6 D3
Gentian Ct. CO4	5 G5
Geoff Seadon Clo. CO1	11 E3
George St. CO1	3 D3
Geranium Walk. CO4	11 F2
Gilberd Rd. CO2	10 D5
Gilderdale Clo. CO4	7 F4
Gilwell Park Clo. CO3	8 D5
Gladstone Rd. CO1	10 C4
Gladiator Way. CO2	12 A2
Gladwin Rd. CO2	9 G5
Glebe Rd. CO2	12 C2
Glen Av. CO3	9 E2
Glendale Gro. CO4	7 E4
Glentrees Clo. CO4	7 F4
Glisson Sq. CO2	9 F6
Gloucester Rd. CO3	9 F6
Goldcrest Clo. CO4	11 H1
Golden Dawn Way. CO4	5 H5
Golden Noble Hill. CO1	10 C4
Goldfinch Clo. CO4	11 H2
Goodey Clo. CO1	10 C4
Goojerat Rd. CO2	10 A5
Goring Rd. CO4	11 E1
Gorse Walk. CO4	11 F2
Gorse Way. CO3	8 B5
Gosbecks Rd. CO2	12 A1
Gosbecks Vw. CO2	12 A2
Gosfield Rd. CO2	13 G4
Grange Way. CO2	11 E6
Grange Way Business Park. CO1	11 E6
Grantham Ct. CO1	3 E3
Grantham Rd. CO6	5 F1
Granville Rd. CO1	10 D4
Granville Rd. CO6	4 C4
Grasby Clo. CO7	15 G2
Grasmere. CO4	6 D3
Gray Rd. CO3	3 A4
Green Acres. CO4	5 H4
Green La. CO6	5 G1
Green La. CO4	7 G5
Greenfinch End. CO4	11 H1
Greenstead Rd. CO1	11 E2
Greenwood Gro. CO4	7 E4
Grenfell Clo. CO4	10 D1
Greyling Dri. CO4	7 G6
Greystones Clo. CO3	8 D6
Grieves Ct. CO3	8 A6
Grimston Rd. CO2	10 C5
Grymes Dyke Way. CO3	8 B6
Guildford Rd. CO1	3 F2
Gurdon Rd. CO2	10 B6
Gurney Benham Clo. CO2	9 E6
Haddon Pk. CO1	11 E3
Hall Rd. CO6	4 B2
Hallcroft Chase. CO4	7 E3
Halstead Rd. CO3	8 A2
Hamilton Rd. CO3	9 G4
Hamilton Rd. CO5	15 G4
Hamlet Dri. CO4	11 G2
Hanbury Gdns. CO4	6 D3
Handy Fisher Ct. CO3	9 E5
Hanningfield Way. CO4	6 D2
Harebell Clo. CO4	6 D4
Harrison Rd. CO2	10 B6
Harsnett Rd. CO1	10 D4
Harvard Ct. CO4	6 D3
Harvest End. CO3	8 B4
Harvey Cres. CO3	8 A5
Harvey Rd. CO2	12 C2
Harvey Rd. CO7	15 G3
Harwich Rd. CO4	11 E2
Harwood Clo. CO2	10 C6
Hastings Rd. CO3	9 E5
Haven Rd. CO2	11 F5
Havering Clo. CO4	6 D6

Hawkins Rd. CO2	11 E3
Hawthorn Av. CO4	11 G3
Hayward Ct. CO4	11 E3
Hazell Av. CO2	12 B1
Hazelton Rd. CO4	7 F6
Head Gate. CO1	3 C4
Head St. CO1	3 C3
Head St. CO5	15 E4
Heath Rd. CO5	15 E4
Heath Rd. CO3	8 B5
Heath Rd. CO3	8 C4
Heath Rd. CO6	4 A5
Heath Rd. CO7	15 G2
Heather Clo. CO2	12 A6
Heather Dri. CO3	8 D4
Heckworth Clo. CO4	7 E2
Hedge Dri. CO2	12 B1
Helm Clo. CO6	5 F1
Henley Clo. CO3	8 C3
Henrietta Clo. CO7	15 H1
Hereford Rd. CO1	3 F2
Hereward Clo. CO7	15 H1
Herrick Pl. CO3	8 D3
Hetherington Clo. CO2	13 G4
Hewes Clo. CO4	11 E2
Hickory Av. CO4	11 F2
High Rd. CO2	12 A6
High St. CO1	3 C3
High St. CO5	15 F4
High St. CO7	15 G4
Highclere Rd. CO4	6 D3
Highfield Dri. CO3	9 G3
Highwoods App. CO4	6 D4
Highwoods Sq. CO4	6 D4
Hilltop Clo. CO1	11 E5
Hill View Clo. CO5	15 E4
Hillridge. CO4	6 D4
Hills Cres. CO3	8 D4
Hillston Clo. CO2	13 G2
Hitherwood Rd. CO2	12 C2
Hoe Dri. CO3	8 D4
Holborough Clo. CO4	11 G2
Holden Rd. CO4	6 B5
Holly Clo. CO2	12 C2
Holly Rd. CO3	8 A5
Hollymead Clo. CO4	6 B4
Hollytree Ct. CO2	9 G6
Holm Oak. CO2	13 G1
Holman Cres. CO3	9 E5
Holt Dri. CO2	13 G5
Homefield Rd. CO2	12 C3
Honeysuckle Way. CO4	11 G1
Honywood Rd. CO6	9 G4
Hornbeam Clo. CO2	12 D2
Horrocks Clo. CO2	10 C6
Hospital La. CO3	3 A4
Hospital Rd. CO3	3 A4
Howards Croft. CO2	5 G3
Howe Clo. CO4	11 F3
Hubert Rd. CO3	9 F2
Hugh Dickson Way. CO4	5 H5
Hunters Ridge. CO4	6 D3
Hunting Gate. CO1	11 E3
Hunting Gate Lodge. CO6	4 D3
Hunwicke Rd. CO4	11 G3
Hurnard Dri. CO3	9 E2
Hurrell Down. CO4	6 C3
Hythe Hill. CO1	11 E3
Hythe Quay. CO2	11 E4
Hythe Station Rd. CO2	11 E3
Iceni Way. CO2	9 F6
Ilex Clo. CO2	12 D2
Imogen Clo. CO4	11 H2
Imphal Rd. CO2	12 C3
INDUSTRIAL ESTATES:	
Grange Way Business Park. CO1	11 E6
Peartree Business Centre. CO3	8 B5
Severalls Ind Est. CO4	7 E2
Whitehall Ind Est. CO1	11 F5
Inglis Rd. CO3	9 G3
Inverness Clo. CO1	3 E2
Inworth Walk. CO2	13 F3
Ipswich Rd. CO4	6 D6
Ireton Rd. CO3	9 G4
Iron Latch La. CO3	8 A1
Irvine Rd. CO3	9 F5
Isbourne Rd. CO3	11 G3
Jack Hatch Way. CO7	15 F1
Jacqueline Ct. CO3	9 E2
James Carter Rd. CO3	8 C6
James Clo. CO7	15 H1
James St. CO1	10 C4
Jarmin Rd. CO1	3 D1
Jasmine Clo. CO4	11 F2
Jefferson Clo. CO3	8 C4
Jeffrey Clo. CO3	8 D4
Jennings Clo. CO4	11 E3
Jessica Clo. CO4	11 H2
John Ball Walk. CO1	3 C2
John Harper St. CO1	3 B1
John Kent Av. CO2	12 B2
Jonquil Way. CO4	5 F5
*Julian Av, Titmus Way. CO4	6 D1
Juniper Rd. CO3	8 A5
Juniper Way. CO4	11 F1
Juno Mews. CO2	12 C3
Kale Croft. CO3	8 B5
Keats Rd. CO3	8 D4
Keble Clo. CO3	9 H3
Keelars Way. CO6	5 E1
Kelso Clo. CO6	5 F1
Kendall Rd. CO1	10 C4
Kentmere. CO4	7 F5
Kerry Ct. CO4	11 E2
Keymer Clo. CO3	8 C5
Kildermorie Clo. CO4	7 F4
Kimberley Rd. CO1	10 D4
King Coel Rd. CO3	8 B2
King Edward Quay. CO1	11 E4
King George Rd. CO2	10 B5
King Harold Rd. CO3	8 D5
King Stephen Rd. CO1	10 D4
Kingfisher Clo. CO4	11 H2
Kings Meadow Rd. CO1	3 C1
Kingswood Rd. CO4	6 B3
Kinlet Clo. CO4	6 D3
Kipling Walk. CO3	8 D3
Kohima Rd. CO2	12 C3
Laburnum Gro. CO4	11 F1
Ladbrook Dri. CO2	10 C6
Ladell Clo. CO3	8 C6
Laing Rd. CO4	11 G3
Lambourne Clo. CO3	8 B5
Lammas Way. CO7	15 H2
Land La. CO1	3 E3
Landseer Rd. CO3	9 F4
Langdale Dri. CO4	6 D3
Langham Pl. CO4	6 D4
Lanvalley Rd. CO3	8 C3
Larch Clo. CO4	11 F1
Launceston Clo. CO2	13 G3
Lavender Way. CO4	5 G5
Laxton Ct. CO3	9 E5
Layer Rd. CO2	12 B6
Le Cateau Rd. CO2	10 A4
Leam Clo. CO4	11 G3
Leas Rd. CO2	12 C3
Leechs La. CO4	5 H3
Leicester Clo. CO1	3 E2
Leith Gro. CO2	13 F4
Lexden Ct. CO3	9 F3
Lexden Gro. CO3	8 D3
Lexden Rd, Colchester. CO3	3 A4
Lexden Rd, Lexden. CO3	8 D3
Lexden Rd. CO6	4 B3
Leys Rd. CO7	15 H1
Lilac Clo. CO7	15 F2
Lime Av. CO4	11 F1
Lincoln Way. CO1	3 E3
Linden Clo. CO4	11 G1
Link Clo. CO4	5 H3
Lion Walk. CO1	3 D3
Lisle Rd. CO2	10 C4
Litchfield Clo. CO1	3 F2
Littlebury Gdns. CO2	11 E6
Littlecotes. CO4	5 G3
Littlefield Rd. CO2	12 C2
Lockhart Av. CO3	9 F3
Lodge Clo. CO6	4 C3
London Rd. CO3	8 A3
Long Wyre St. CO1	3 D3
Longacre. CO4	5 H5
Longcroft Rd. CO4	11 E2
Longedryve. CO2	9 G5
Longridge. CO4	11 H1
Longstraw Clo. CO3	8 B4
Lord Holland Rd. CO2	10 B6
Lordswood Rd. CO2	12 C2
Lucas Rd. CO2	10 B4
Lucy Clo. CO3	8 A3
Lucy Lane Sth. CO3	8 A3
Lufkin Rd. CO4	6 B4
Lugar Clo. CO4	11 G3
Mabbitt Way. CO4	6 D2
Macbeth Clo. CO4	11 H2
Mackay Ct. CO2	13 G3
Magazine Farm Way. CO3	9 E4
Magdalen Grn. CO1	3 F4
Magdalen St. CO1	3 E4
Magnolia Dri. CO4	11 G2
Maidenburgh St. CO1	3 D2
Maldon Rd. CO3	3 B4
Maldon Rd. CO2	12 A1
Malting Rd. CO2	12 C3
Maltings Pl. CO6	4 D3
Maltings Yd. CO7	15 G4
Manor Rd. CO3	3 A4
Manor Rd. CO6	4 C3
Manor Rd. CO7	15 H3
Maple Way. CO2	10 C5
Marasca End. CO2	13 G5
Maraschino Cres. CO2	13 G5
Mareth Rd. CO2	12 C2
Margaret Rd. CO1	3 C1
Marigold Clo. CO4	11 G2
Marlowe Way. CO3	8 D3
Marne Rd. CO2	10 A6
Marram Clo. CO3	8 A3
Marsh Cres. CO5	15 F4
Maryborough Gro. CO2	13 G2
Maryland Ct. CO2	13 G3
Masefield Dri. CO3	8 D3
Mason Clo. CO2	9 F6
Mason Rd. CO1	3 D1
Maudlyn Rd. CO1	11 E4
Mayberry Walk. CO2	13 F1
Mayfield Clo. CO4	7 E6
Mayflower Clo. CO3	8 B3
Maypole Green Rd. CO2	12 C3
Meadow Rd. CO2	12 D3
Meadow View Clo. CO3	8 B4
Meadowbrook Ct. CO1	3 F4
Mede Way. CO7	15 H1
Melbourne Clo. CO2	13 G3
Mellor Chase. CO3	8 C2
Menin Rd. CO2	9 G5
Mercers Way. CO1	3 C1
Mercury Clo. CO2	12 A1
Merlin End. CO4	11 H1
Mersea Rd. CO2	10 B3
Merton Ct. CO2	13 G5
Messines Rd. CO2	9 G5
Meyrick Cres. CO2	10 B5
Middle Mill Rd. CO1	3 D2
Middleborough. CO1	3 C2
Middlewick Clo. CO2	13 F3
Midland Clo. CO2	10 B5
Midway Rd. CO2	12 C2
Mile End Rd. CO4	5 H3
Miles Clo. CO3	8 A3
Milford Rd. CO7	15 H3
Military Rd. CO1	3 E4
Mill Rd. CO4	5 H3
Mill St. CO1	10 C4
Millers Clo. CO3	8 A3
Millers La. CO3	8 B3
Milton Clo. CO3	8 D4
Minerva End. CO2	12 C3
Monkwick Av. CO2	13 F3
Mons Rd. CO2	9 G5
Montbretia Clo. CO3	8 B3
Montgomery Clo. CO2	10 C5
Moorside. CO4	10 D2
Morant Rd. CO1	10 D4
Morello Ct. CO2	13 G5
Morten Rd. CO1	3 B1
Moss Way. CO3	8 C5
Moss Way. CO6	4 C4
Mossfield Clo. CO3	9 F3
Mountain Ash Clo. CO4	7 E5
Mountbatten Dri. CO2	10 D6
Moy Rd. CO2	13 F3
Mulberry Av. CO2	10 C6
Mumford Clo. CO6	4 B3
Mumford Rd. CO6	4 B4
Munnings Rd. CO3	9 E5
Museum St. CO1	3 D3
Musk Clo. CO3	8 B3
Myrtle Gro. CO2	10 C4
Nancy Smith Clo. CO2	10 B5
Napier Rd. CO2	10 B4
Nash Clo. CO3	9 E4
Nathan Ct. CO2	14 A4
Nayland Rd. CO4	5 G1
Nayland Rd. CO6	4 B2
Nelson Rd. CO3	8 C3
New Church Rd. CO6	4 B3
New Cut. CO2	12 A6
New Farm Rd. CO3	8 B4
New Kiln Rd. CO3	9 G2
New Park St. CO1	10 D4
New Rd. CO3	8 B3
New Town Rd. CO1	10 C4
Newbridge Hill. CO3	4 B5
Newcastle Av. CO3	8 C6
Newcomen Way. CO4	7 E1
Nicholsons Gro. CO1	3 E4
Nightingale Clo. CO4	11 H2
Norfolk Cres. CO4	6 D6
Norman Way. CO3	9 F1
Norman Way. CO3	9 F5
Normandy Av. CO2	10 C6
North Hill. CO1	3 C2
North Station Rd. CO1	3 B1
Northern By-Pass. CO4	5 E4
Northfield Gdns. CO4	6 C3
Northgate St. CO1	3 C2
Norwich Clo. CO1	3 E2
Nunns Rd. CO1	3 C1
Nursery Clo. CO3	8 A4
Oakapple Clo. CO2	12 D3
Oaklands Av. CO3	8 C5
Oaks Clo. CO6	4 C4
Oaks Dri. CO3	3 A4
Oaks Pl. CO4	6 A4
Oatfield Clo. CO3	8 B4
Oberon Clo. CO4	11 H2
Old Coach Rd. CO4	10 D2
Old Heath Rd. CO1	11 E5
Old Rose Gdns. CO4	5 H4
Olivers La. CO2	12 A4
Onslow Cres. CO2	13 G3
Orchard Gdns. CO4	10 D7
Orchard Rd. CO1	3 B1
Ormonde Clo. CO6	4 C5
Orpen Clo. CO6	4 B3
Orwell Clo. CO4	7 G6
Osborne St. CO2	3 D4
Othello Clo. CO4	11 H2
Owenward Clo. CO2	9 E6
Owls Retreat. CO4	11 H1
Oxford Rd. CO3	3 A4
Paddock Way. CO7	15 H1
Paget Rd. CO5	15 E4
Paget Rd. CO7	15 G4
Pampas Clo. CO4	6 C3
Panton Cres. CO4	11 G3
Papillon Rd. CO3	3 A3
Park Rd CO4	11 H5
Park Rd. CO3	9 F3
Park Rd. CO7	15 G4
Parkfield St. CO5	15 E5
Parkwood Av. CO7	15 G3
Parnell Clo. CO2	13 G5
Parr Dri. CO3	3 C6
Parsons Heath. CO4	7 G6
Parsons Hill. CO3	8 D6
Parsons La. CO1	11 E3
Patmore Rd. CO4	11 F3
Paul Spendlove Ct. CO4	7 G6
Paxman Av. CO2	9 E6
Peace Rd. CO3	8 A3
Pearmain Way. CO3	8 A4
Peartree Business Centre. CO3	8 B5
Peartree Rd. CO3	8 B5
Pebmarsh Clo. CO2	13 G3
Pedlers Clo. CO2	12 A4
Peerswood Rd. CO2	12 D2
Pegasus Way. CO4	7 E5
Pelhams La. CO1	3 C3
Pembroke Clo. CO2	10 D7
Penrice Clo. CO4	11 F3
Peregrine Ct. CO4	11 H3
Persardi Ct. CO2	13 G3
Pershore End. CO3	8 C4
Perth Clo. CO2	13 G5
Petworth Clo. CO7	15 H5
Peto Av. CO4	6 B6
Phillip Rd. CO7	15 G4
Pickford Walk. CO4	11 G5
Pilborough Way. CO3	8 C7

e Ct. CO7	15 G4
hecroft Gdns. CO4	6 D4
ber Rd. CO3	9 F2
ie Rd. CO6	4 C3
ains Farm Clo. CO7	7 F1
ough Dri. CO3	8 D4
oughmans Headland. CO3	8 B4
ume Av. CO3	9 E5
ndfield Rd. CO4	7 F6
eperinghe Rd. CO2	10 B5
pes La. CO3	3 B3
ppy Gdns. CO2	10 D6
rt La. CO1	10 D4
rters Brook Walk. CO4	7 E5
rtland Rd. CO2	10 B3
sford Ct. CO4	6 B3
wnall Cres. CO2	10 B5
esident Rd. CO3	8 C4
ettygate Rd. CO3	9 E4
rimrose Walk. CO4	11 G2
ince Charles Rd. CO2	13 F2
ince Philip Rd. CO2	13 F3
inceton Mews. CO4	6 D3
ory St. CO1	3 D4
ory Walk. CO1	3 D3
ory Way. CO4	6 A5
ospero Clo. CO4	11 G2
ovence Clo. CO3	8 A3
unus Ct. CO2	13 G5
rcell Clo. CO4	11 G3
rvis Way. CO4	6 D2
efleet Clo. CO5	15 G6
uakers Alley. CO1	3 C3
uay St. CO7	15 G4
ueen Elizabeth Way. CO2	13 G3
ueen Mary Av. CO2	10 B5
ueen St. CO1	3 D4
ueens Rd. CO3	9 G4
ueens Rd. CO6	4 B4
ueens Rd. CO7	15 G4
ueensland Dri. CO2	13 G3
insborowe Rd. CO2	9 G6
mbler Clo. CO3	8 B3
mparts Ct. CO4	5 E5
nger Walk. CO2	10 D6
ngoon Clo. CO2	12 C3
tcliffe Rd. CO3	8 C4
ven Way. CO4	6 A3
wlings Cres. CO4	6 D2
wstorn Rd. CO3	3 B3
yleigh Clo. CO4	10 D1
yner Rd. CO2	9 E6
aper Rd. CO3	8 D5
bow Rd. CO7	15 G4
bow St. CO1	10 D4
creation Rd. CO1	10 D5
ctory Clo. CO4	5 H5
ctory Clo. CO7	15 H3
ctory Hill. CO7	15 H3
ctory Rd. CO5	14 D4
ctory Rd. CO7	15 H2
d Lion Yd. CO1	3 D3
dmill. CO3	9 E6
dwood Clo. CO4	11 F1
ed Hall Av Nth. CO2	9 G6
ed Hall Av Sth. CO2	12 C1
gency Grn. CO3	8 D5
gent Hill. CO5	15 F4
gents Clo. CO4	7 E2
mbrandt Way. CO3	9 F4
mus Clo. CO4	6 B2
ynards Copse. CO4	6 C4
ynolds Av. CO3	9 F5
chard Av. CO7	15 H1
chardson Walk. CO3	8 D4
ddles Dri. CO4	6 B5
dgeway. CO4	6 C4
dgewell Way. CO2	13 F3
pple Way. CO4	10 D1
ach Vale. CO4	7 G6
bert Way. CO7	15 H1
berts Rd. CO2	10 C4
chdale Way. CO4	11 F3
ckhampton Walk. CO2	13 G3
ckingham Clo. CO4	7 E4
ddam Clo. CO3	9 F3
gation Clo. CO3	8 B4
man Hill. CO2	13 H5
man Rd. CO1	3 E2
man Way. CO2	13 E3
Romford Clo. CO4	10 D1
Romulus Clo. CO4	6 B2
Roosevelt Way. CO2	10 D5
Rosabelle Av. CO7	15 G3
Rosalind Clo. CO4	11 G2
Rose Av. CO3	8 A5
Rose Cres. CO4	5 H5
Rose Ct. CO3	13 G4
Rose La. CO7	15 G5
Rosebery Av. CO1	3 F3
Rosendale Clo. CO4	7 E4
Rossetta Clo. CO7	15 F2
Rosewood Clo. CO4	6 C3
Round Clo. CO3	9 F2
Rowallan Clo. CO3	8 D6
Rowan Clo. CO3	8 B5
Rowhedge Ferry Rd. CO7	15 F4
Rowhedge Rd. CO2	14 C2
Royal Ct. CO4	7 F6
Rudd Ct. CO4	7 G6
Rudkin Rd. CO4	6 B3
Rudsdale Way. CO3	8 D4
Rugosa Clo. CO3	8 A3
Rutland Av. CO2	9 F6
Rye Clo. CO7	8 B4
Ryegate Rd. CO1	3 D2
Sackville Way. CO6	4 B3
Saddle Mews. CO3	8 B3
Sadler Clo. CO2	10 D5
Sage Rd. CO2	13 G2
St Albans Rd. CO3	3 A3
St Andrews Av. CO4	10 D2
St Andrews Gdns. CO4	10 D2
St Annes Rd. CO4	10 D1
St Austell Rd. CO4	7 F5
St Barbaras Rd. CO2	9 G5
St Bartholomew Clo. CO4	7 E4
St Bernard Rd. CO4	7 F5
St Botolphs St. CO2	3 D4
St Bride Clo. CO4	7 F5
St Catherines Clo. CO2	12 D3
St Christpher Rd. CO4	7 E5
St Clare Dri. CO3	9 E3
St Clare Rd. CO3	9 E3
St Clement Rd. CO4	7 F5
St Columb Ct. CO4	7 E5
St Cyrus Rd. CO4	7 E5
St Davids Clo. CO4	11 E2
St Dominics Rd. CO4	11 E6
St Edmunds Ct. CO4	11 E2
St Faith Rd. CO4	7 F5
St Fillan Rd. CO4	7 E6
St Helena Rd. CO3	9 G4
St Helens La. CO1	3 D3
St Johns Av. CO2	3 C4
St Johns Clo. CO4	7 E3
St Johns Grn. CO2	3 D4
St Johns Rd. CO4	7 E4
St Johns Rd. CO7	15 G4
St Johns St. CO2	3 C4
St Joseph Rd. CO4	7 E5
St Jude Clo. CO4	7 F5
St Jude Gdns. CO4	7 F5
St Julian Gro. CO1	3 E4
St Lawrence Rd. CO4	7 F5
St Leonards Rd. CO1	10 D4
St Luke Clo. CO4	7 F5
St Mark Dri. CO4	7 E5
St Michaels Rd. CO2	12 D3
St Monance Way. CO4	7 F5
St Neots Clo. CO4	7 F5
St Nicholas St. CO1	3 D3
St Pauls Rd. CO1	3 B1
St Peters St. CO1	3 C2
St Runwald St. CO1	3 C3
St Savior Clo. CO4	7 F5
St Thomass Clo. CO4	7 G5
Salary Clo. CO4	11 G1
Salerno Cres. CO2	12 C2
Salisbury Av. CO3	10 A4
Salmon Clo. CO3	8 C5
Sanders Dri. CO3	9 F2
Sanderson Ct. CO1	3 C3
Sandpiper Clo. CO4	11 H2
Sandringham Dri. CO2	10 C5
Saran Ct. CO7	15 F2
Sargeant Clo. CO2	10 D6
Savill Rd. CO2	14 C2
Saxon Clo. CO3	8 D5
Scarfe Way. CO4	11 G3
Scarletts Rd. CO1	10 D5
Scheregate. CO2	3 C4
School La. CO6	4 C3
School Rd. CO2	13 F2
Scott Dri. CO3	8 D4
Scythe Way. CO3	8 D5
Seaking Cres. CO4	6 D3
Sebastian Clo. CO4	11 G2
Serpentine Walk. CO1	3 C1
Severalls Ind Est. CO4	7 E2
Severalls La. CO4	6 D1
Sexton Clo. CO2	13 G4
Shakespeare Rd. CO3	8 D3
Shearwater Mews. CO4	11 H1
Sheepen Pl. CO3	3 B2
Sheepen Rd. CO3	3 A2
Sheering Walk. CO2	13 F2
Shelley Rd. CO3	8 C3
Shepherds Croft. CO3	8 B4
Sherbourne Rd. CO4	11 H3
Sheridan Walk. CO3	8 C3
Sherwood Clo. CO4	11 F3
Shewell Walk. CO1	3 C3
Shillito Clo. CO4	8 C6
Short Cut Rd. CO1	3 C2
Short Wyre St. CO1	3 D4
Shrub End Rd. CO3	9 E6
Siena Mews. CO2	10 D6
Silcock Clo. CO4	7 E5
Silvanus Clo. CO3	9 G3
Silverthorne Clo. CO2	13 G1
Simons La. CO1	3 F4
Sinclair Clo. CO4	6 B5
Sinnington End. CO4	7 E3
Sioux Clo. CO4	6 D3
Sir Isaacs Walk. CO1	3 C4
Siskin Clo. CO4	11 H2
Sittang Clo. CO2	12 C3
Smallwood Rd. CO2	12 B1
Smeaton Clo. CO4	7 E2
Smiths Field. CO1	11 E5
Smythies Av. CO1	3 F3
Snowberry Gro. CO2	13 G1
Somers Rd. CO3	9 E6
Somerset Clo. CO2	9 F6
Somme Rd. CO2	10 A6
Sonnell Ct. CO7	15 F2
Sorrell Clo. CO4	5 F5
South St. CO2	3 C4
Southland Clo. CO4	7 E6
Southway. CO2	3 C4
Sparling Clo. CO2	12 C2
Speedwell Rd. CO2	14 C2
Spindle Wood. CO4	6 C3
Sports Way. CO1	3 D1
Spring Chase. CO7	15 G2
Spring Clo. CO4	6 D4
Spring La. CO5	15 G6
Spring La. CO3	8 D2
Spring La. CO6	4 B4
Spring La. CO7	15 F2
Spring Sedge Clo. CO3	8 A3
Springfield Dri. CO2	12 A1
Spruce Av. CO4	11 F1
Spurgeon St. CO1	11 E3
Squirrels Field. CO4	6 B2
Stable Clo. CO3	8 B3
Stalin Rd. CO2	10 C5
Stammers Rd. CO4	6 B3
*Standard Rd, St Leonards Rd. CO1	10 D4
Stanfield Clo. CO3	8 C6
Stanley Rd. CO7	15 G3
Stanley Wooster Way. CO4	11 G3
Stansted Rd. CO2	13 G3
Stanwell St. CO2	3 D4
Station Rd. CO7	15 G4
Station Way. CO1	3 C4
Stephen Cranfield Clo .CO5	15 F4
Stephenson Rd. CO4	7 E2
Sterling Clo. CO3	8 C4
Stirrup Mews. CO3	8 B3
Stockwell St. CO1	3 C3
Stonecrop. CO4	5 G5
Stoneleigh Park. CO3	8 D6
Stow Ct. CO4	6 B3
Straight Rd. CO3	8 C3
Studds La. CO4	5 H3
Suffolk Clo. CO4	6 D6
Sullivan Clo. CO4	11 F4
Sussex Rd. CO3	9 G3
Sutton Park Av. CO3	8 D6
Swallowdale. CO2	11 E6
Swan Clo. CO4	11 F4
Swan Pass. CO1	3 D3
Sweet Briar Rd. CO3	8 A3
Sycamore Rd. CO4	11 F1
Sydney St. CO2	13 G3
Tabor Clo. CO4	11 E3
Talcott Rd. CO2	13 G2
Tall Trees. CO4	6 A4
Tally Ho. CO4	6 D3
Tamworth Chase. CO2	13 G2
Tangerine Clo. CO4	11 F3
Tapwoods. CO3	9 E2
Tara Clo. CO4	11 F1
Tarragona Mews. CO2	10 D6
Taylor Ct. CO1	3 D3
Taylors Rd. CO5	15 E4
Tedder Clo. CO2	10 C6
Telford Rd. CO4	7 E2
Temple Ct. CO4	7 F5
Temple Rd. CO2	12 A2
Templewood Rd. CO4	7 F6
Terling Clo. CO2	13 G3
Terrace Hall Chase. CO6	5 G1
Thaxted Walk. CO2	13 G4
The Avenue. CO3	9 G3
The Avenue. CO6	4 B4
The Avenue. CO7	15 G3
The Brackens. CO4	6 D5
The Brambles. CO3	8 D6
The Causeway. CO4	7 E5
The Chantry. CO2	9 F2
The Chase. CO3	8 C3
The Chase Way. CO3	9 F1
The Commons. CO3	8 D4
The Copse. CO4	6 B4
The Crescent. CO4	6 D1
The Dale. CO7	15 H4
The Dell. CO1	3 E4
The Folly. CO2	12 B6
The Folly. CO7	15 G5
The Glade. CO4	7 G6
The Haywain. CO3	8 B4
The Jays. CO4	6 D4
The Mount. CO3	8 D3
The Nook. CO7	15 H4
The Quay. CO7	15 G5
The Retreat. CO6	4 B4
The Square. CO2	12 B1
The Trueman. CO6	4 D3
The Willows. CO2	10 C6
Thistledown. CO4	6 D4
Thomas Wakley Clo. CO4	6 B2
Thompson Av. CO3	8 D3
Thornton Dri. CO4	6 B5
Thornwood. CO4	6 B5
Thracian Clo. CO2	12 A2
Three Crowns Rd. CO4	5 H6
Thurlston Clo. CO4	7 F6
Timber Hill. CO1	11 E3
Tippett Clo. CO4	11 F3
Titania Clo. CO4	11 H2
Titmus Way. CO4	6 D1
Tobruk Rd. CO6	9 G6
Toga Clo. CO4	12 A2
Tollgate Dri. CO3	8 A3
Tollgate East. CO3	8 A3
Tollgate Rd. CO3	8 A5
Tollgate West. CO3	8 A4
Tolliday Clo. CO7	15 F2
Tony Webb Clo. CO4	6 D3
Tortosa Clo. CO4	10 D6
Tower Rd. CO7	15 G2
Trafalgar Rd. CO3	8 C3
Trinity Clo. CO7	15 H3
Trinity St. CO1	3 C3
Trojan Clo. CO4	6 D1
Tudor Rose Clo. CO3	8 A2
Tufnell Way. CO4	5 C5
Tulip Walk. CO4	11 E2
Turner Ct. CO7	15 H3
Turner Rd. CO4	6 B3
Turnstone End. CO4	11 H2
Tussett Mews. CO3	8 C2
Twining Rd. CO3	8 C5
Tydeman Clo. CO3	8 A6
Tyehurst Cres. CO4	7 E5
Tynedale Sq. CO4	6 D3
Unity Clo. CO2	10 D5
Upland Dri. CO4	7 E5

Upton Clo. CO6 — 4 B4
Vale Clo. CO4 — 7 F5
Valentines Dri. CO4 — 10 D1
Valfreda Way. CO7 — 15 G2
Valley Clo. CO3 — 8 C6
Valley Cres. CO6 — 4 C4
Valley Rd. CO4 — 11 G5
Valley Rd. CO7 — 15 H4
Valley Vw. CP4 — 4 C4
Valleyview Clo. CO4 — 6 C4
Van Dyck Rd. CO3 — 9 E4
Vanessa Dri. CO7 — 15 G3
Viceroy Clo. CO2 — 10 D6
Victor Rd. CO1 — 10 D4
Victoria Chase. CO1 — 3 B1
Victoria Clo. CO7 — 15 G2
Victoria Gdns. CO4 — 6 D4
Victoria Pl. CO1 — 3 D4
Victoria Rd. CO3 — 9 G4
Villa Rd. CO3 — 8 A3
Vine Dri. CO7 — 15 H1
Vine Farm Rd. CO7 — 15 H1
Vineyard St. CO2 — 3 D4
Vint Cres. CO3 — 9 G3
Viola Walk. CO4 — 11 G2
Viscount Dri. CO4 — 7 E3
Wakefield Clo. CO1 — 3 E2
Wallis Ct. CO3 — 8 C6
Walnut Tree Way. CO2 — 9 E6
Walsingham Rd. CO2 — 3 C4
Walter Radcliffe Way. CO7 — 15 H5
Walters Yd. CO1 — 3 C3
Warren La. CO3 — 8 A6
Washington Ct. CO3 — 8 C4
Wat Tyler Walk. CO1 — 3 C2
Water La. CO3 — 9 G1
Waterville Mews. CO2 — 10 D6
Watts Rd. CO2 — 12 B2
Wavell Av. CO2 — 9 G5
Weavers Clo. CO3 — 8 D5
Wedgewood Dri. CO4 — 6 A5
Weir La. CO2 — 13 H5
Wellesley Rd. CO3 — 3 B4
Wellington St. CO2 — 3 C4
Wells Rd. CO1 — 3 F2
Welshwood Park Rd. CO4 — 7 G5
Wesley Av. CO4 — 11 E2
West Lodge Rd. CO3 — 9 G3
West Stockwell. CO1 — 3 C2
West St. CO2 — 3 C4
West St. CO5 — 15 E4
West St. CO7 — 15 G4
West View Clo. CO4 — 6 D4
West Wood Hill. CO4 — 5 E4
Westlake Cres. CO7 — 15 F2
Weston Rd. CO2 — 10 D5
Westway. CO1 — 3 B1
Wethersfield Rd. CO2 — 13 G4
Wetzlar Ct. CO2 — 10 D6
Whaley Rd. CO4 — 11 E2
Wheatfield Rd. CO3 — 8 B4
Wheeler Clo. CO4 — 11 G3
White Friars Way. CO3 — 9 E4
White Hart La. CO6 — 4 B2
Whitehall Clo. CO4 — 11 E6
Whitehall Ind Est. CO1 — 11 F5
Whitehall Rd. CO2 — 11 E6
Whitehouse La. CO6 — 4 B5
Whitwell Rd. CO2 — 3 D4
Wick Rd. CO2 — 14 C2
Wickham Rd. CO3 — 10 A4
Wilkin Ct. CO3 — 9 E6
Willett Rd. CO2 — 9 F6
William Bovs Clo. CO4 — 11 F1
Williams Walk. CO1 — 3 D3
Willingham Way. CO4 — 11 G2
Willow Clo. CO4 — 7 F1
Wilmington Rd. CO4 — 7 E5
Wilson Clo. CO7 — 15 F2
Wilson Marriage Rd. CO4 — 7 E6
Wimpole Rd. CO1 — 10 D4
Winchester Rd. CO2 — 10 C4
Windsor Clo. CO2 — 13 G2
Winnock Rd. CO1 — 10 C4
Winsley Rd. CO1 — 10 C4
Winsley Sq. CO1 — 10 D5
Winston Av. CO3 — 9 E5
Winstree Rd. CO3 — 8 B4
Wivenhoe Cross. CO7 — 15 G2
Wolfe Av. CO1 — 10 C4
Wolton Rd. CO2 — 12 B1

Woodcock Clo. CO4 — 11 G3
Woodland Way. CO7 — 15 G3
Woodlands. CO4 — 7 G5
Woodpecker Clo. CO4 — 11 H1
Woodrow Way. CO4 — 11 G3
Woodrush End. CO3 — 8 D3
Woodside Clo. CO4 — 7 F6
Woodview Clo. CO4 — 7 F3
Worcester Rd. CO1 — 3 E2
Wordsworth Rd. CO3 — 8 D3
Worthington Way. CO3 — 8 D5
Wroxham Clo. CO3 — 9 F3
Wryneck Clo. CO4 — 6 B4
Wych Elm. CO2 — 13 C1
Wycliffe Gro. CO1 — 6 A6
Wycolls Rd. CO4 — 7 E3
Wyedale Dri. CO3 — 8 C4
Wyndham Clo. CO2 — 13 G4
Yale Mews. CO4 — 6 D3
Yew Tree Clo. CO4 — 11 G2
York Pl. CO1 — 3 F2
Ypres Rd. CO2 — 10 A6

HALSTEAD

Abels Rd. CO9 — 25 A5
Acorn Av. CO9 — 25 A4
Adams Ct. CO9 — 25 A3
Apple Tree Clo. CO9 — 25 D2
Ashlong Cres. CO9 — 25 B1
Balls Chase. CO9 — 25 C4
Beech Av. CO9 — 25 D3
Beridge Rd. CO9 — 25 A2
Blamsters Cres. CO9 — 25 A5
Bois Field Ter. CO9 — 25 B3
Bois Hall Gdns. CO9 — 25 C2
Bourchier Way. CO9 — 25 A4
Bourne Clo. CO9 — 25 A5
Box Mill La. CO9 — 25 B2
Bridge St. CO9 — 25 B3
Brook Farm Clo. CO9 — 25 D4
Broton Dri. CO9 — 25 B3
Butler Rd. CO9 — 25 A3
Causeway. CO9 — 25 B3
Chapel Hill. CO9 — 25 A3
Chapel Street. CO9 — 25 B3
Cherry Tree Clo. CO9 — 25 D3
Chipping Hill. CO9 — 25 C3
Churchill Av. CO9 — 25 C2
Clare Clo. CO9 — 25 B5
*Clovers,
  Oxford Rd. CO9 — 25 A4
Coggeshall Pieces. CO9 — 25 D3
Coggeshall Way. CO9 — 25 D3
Colchester Rd. CO9 — 25 C3
Colne Rd. CO9 — 25 C2
Colne Valley Clo. CO9 — 25 A3
Conies Rd. CO9 — 25 A5
Conway Clo. CO9 — 25 A5
Cooks Clo. CO9 — 25 C5
Courtauld Clo. CO9 — 25 C4
Courtlands, Abels Rd. CO9 — 25 A5
Cutting Dri. CO9 — 25 B4
De Veres Ct. CO9 — 25 A4
Dooley Rd. CO9 — 25 A3
Dorset Clo. CO9 — 25 B4
East Mill. CO9 — 25 C3
Elizabeth Way. CO9 — 25 B3
Elm Dri. CO9 — 25 C4
Factory Lane East. CO9 — 25 B3
Factory Lane West. CO9 — 25 B4
Fairfield Way. CO9 — 25 C4
Fenn Rd. CO9 — 25 D3
Finsbury Pl. CO9 — 25 C3
Firwoods Rd. CO9 — 25 B5
Fleece Yd. CO9 — 25 B3
Gardeners Rd. CO9 — 25 C4
Gatehouse Yd. CO9 — 25 B3
Godwin Clo. CO9 — 25 A4
Grange Clo. CO9 — 25 B6
Great Yard. CO9 — 25 B5
Harold Clo. CO9 — 25 C3
Harvey St. CO9 — 25 C3
Haubourdin Ct. CO9 — 25 D3
Hawthorn Clo. CO9 — 25 D3
Head St. CO9 — 25 C3
Hedingham Rd. CO9 — 25 A1
High St. CO9 — 25 B3
Highbury Ter. CO9 — 25 C3

Highfields. CO9 — 25 B5
Holman Rd. CO9 — 25 B4
Holmes Rd. CO9 — 25 B5
Honeywood Rd. CO9 — 25 C2
Howe Chase. CO9 — 25 B1
Johnson Clo. CO9 — 25 C4
Juniper Clo. CO9 — 25 A3
Kings Rd. CO9 — 25 B3
Knowles Clo. CO9 — 25 B4
Link Rd. CO9 — 25 A5
Lock Rd. CO9 — 25 B5
Mallows Field. CO9 — 25 C3
Manfield. CO9 — 25 C3
Maple Clo. CO9 — 25 D3
Mathews Clo. CO9 — 25 D2
Mayda Clo. CO9 — 25 B4
Meadow Clo. CO9 — 25 C4
Middlefield. CO9 — 25 C3
Mill Bridge. CO9 — 25 B3
Mill Chase. CO9 — 25 B2
Mitchell Av. CO9 — 25 B4
Monklands Ct. CO9 — 25 A4
Morley Rd. CO9 — 25 C3
Morton Way. CO9 — 25 D1
Mount Clo. CO9 — 25 A4
Mount Hill. CO9 — 25 A5
Mount Pleasant. CO9 — 25 B4
Neale St. CO9 — 25 B4
Nether Ct. CO9 — 25 C3
New St. CO9 — 25 B3
North Mill Pl. CO9 — 25 B2
Oak Rd. CO9 — 25 A5
Orchard Av. CO9 — 25 A3
Oxford Rd. CO9 — 25 A4
Park Dri. CO9 — 25 B4
Parker Way. CO9 — 25 B5
Parsonage St. CO9 — 25 C4
Paynters Ter. CO9 — 25 C3
Poplar Clo. CO9 — 25 C4
Portway Ct. CO9 — 25 C2
Pretoria Rd. CO9 — 25 C3
Prior Clo. CO9 — 25 A4
Ramsey Rd. CO9 — 25 A4
Ravens Av. CO9 — 25 C4
Rayner Way. CO9 — 25 B4
River Clo. CO9 — 25 C4
Ronald Rd. CO9 — 25 B5
Rose Yd. CO9 — 25 C3
Rosemary La. CO9 — 25 B3
Roundacre. CO9 — 25 B5
St Andrews Rd. CO9 — 25 C3
Saxon Clo. CO9 — 25 C3
Saxon Way. CO9 — 25 C3
School Chase. CO9 — 25 B4
Slate. CO9 — 25 C4
Sloe Hill. CO9 — 25 A3
Slough Farm Rd. CO9 — 25 A3
South Clo. CO9 — 25 B5
Spansey Ct. CO9 — 25 A4
Stanley Rd. CO9 — 25 A3
Stanstead Rd. CO9 — 25 C5
Sudbury Rd. CO9 — 25 C2
Symonds Ct. CO9 — 25 C3
The Centre. CO9 — 25 B3
The Pippins. CO9 — 25 A3
The Tythings. CO9 — 25 A4
Three Gates Clo. CO9 — 25 A5
Tidings Hill. CO9 — 25 B6
Trinity Ct. CO9 — 25 B3
Trinity Rd. CO9 — 25 A4
Trinity St. CO9 — 25 A3
Tryon Ct. CO9 — 25 A4
Tweed Clo. CO9 — 25 A5
Tylneys Rd. CO9 — 25 C2
Upper Chapel St. CO9 — 25 B3
Upper Fenn Rd. CO9 — 25 D3
Upper Trinity Rd. CO9 — 25 B4
Vicarage Ct. CO9 — 25 A3
Vicarage Meadow. CO9 — 25 B3
Warren Rd. CO9 — 25 A4
Weavers Row. CO9 — 25 C3
Well Field. CO9 — 25 C5
West Rd. CO9 — 25 B4
West Yard. CO9 — 25 B4
White Horse Av. CO9 — 25 A5
Willow Way. CO9 — 25 A4
Windmill Rd. CO9 — 25 A4
Winston Way. CO9 — 25 D2

HARWICH

Abbott Rd. CO12 — 16 D
Abdy Av. CO12 — 16 B
Acorn Clo. CO12 — 16 D
Adelaide St. CO12 — 16 C
Ainger Rd. CO12 — 16 C
Albermarle St. CO12 — 17 G
Albert St. CO12 — 17 G
Aldon Clo. CO12 — 16 A
Alexandra Rd. CO12 — 17 G
Alexandra St. CO12 — 17 G
Allfields. CO12 — 16 D
Angel Gate. CO12 — 17 H
Anson Clo. CO12 — 16 D
Arderne Clo. CO12 — 16 C
Ashley Rd. CO12 — 17 E
Bagshaw Rd. CO12 — 17 G
Balton Way. CO12 — 16 D
Barrack La. CO12 — 17 H
Bay Rd. CO12 — 17 G
Beach Rd. CO12 — 17 F
Beacon Hill Av. CO12 — 17 H
Beryl Rd. CO12 — 16 E
Bexley Av. CO12 — 16 C
Birch Av. CO12 — 17 F
Blackthorne La. CO12 — 16 D
Briardale Av. CO12 — 16 D
Brooklyn Rd. CO12 — 17 G
Bruges Clo. CO12 — 17 F
Brussels Clo. CO12 — 17 F
Burr Clo. CO12 — 16 A
Canning St. CO12 — 17 G
Castle Gate St. CO12 — 17 H
Chase La. CO12 — 16 G
Chevy Ct. CO12 — 16 A
Church St. CO12 — 17 G
Clarkes Rd. CO12 — 16 D
Clayton Rd. CO12 — 16 A
Cliff Rd. CO12 — 17 G
Coke St. CO12 — 17 G
Coller Rd. CO12 — 16 G
Cooks Clo. CO12 — 16 D
Cow La. CO12 — 17 H
*Crown La,
  High St. CO12 — 17 G
Currents La. CO12 — 17 H
Davall Clo. CO12 — 16 A
De Vere Way. CO12 — 16 G
Deanes Clo. CO12 — 16 D
Deanes La. CO12 — 16 I
Deepdale Rd. CO12 — 17 E
Devon Way. CO12 — 16 I
Dockfield Av. CO12 — 16 C
Douglas Rd. CO12 — 17 E
Dove Cres. CO12 — 16 I
Dovercourt By-Pass. CO12 — 16 A
Earlham Clo. CO12 — 16 G
East Dock Rd. CO12 — 16 G
East St. CO12 — 17 G
Easterling Clo. CO12 — 17 E
Eastgate St. CO12 — 17 H
Edward St. CO12 — 16 G
Elizabeth Rd. CO12 — 17 I
Elm Dri. CO12 — 17 I
Elmhurst Rd. CO12 — 17 G
Empire Rd. CO12 — 17 G
Europa Way. CO12 — 16 D
Eves Ct. CO12 — 16 E
Fallowfield Clo. CO12 — 16 D
Ferndale Rd. CO12 — 17 G
Fernlea Rd. CO12 — 17 G
First Av. CO12 — 17 I
Foster Rd. CO12 — 16 I
Freshfields. CO12 — 16 I
Frobisher Rd. CO12 — 16 I
Fronks Av. CO12 — 16 I
Fronks Rd. CO12 — 16 I
Fryatt Av. CO12 — 16 I
Garland Rd. CO12 — 16 I
George St. CO12 — 17 I
Goodlake Clo. CO12 — 16 I
Gordon Rd. CO12 — 17
Gordon Way. CO12 — 17
Grafton Rd. CO12 — 17 I
Grange Rd. CO12 — 17 I
Gravel Hill Way. CO12 — 16 I
Gwynne Rd. CO12 — 17 I

Gypsy La. CO12   16 B6
Halfacre La. CO12   16 D5
Hall La. CO12   17 E5
Hamilton St. CO12   16 D2
Hankin Av. CO12   16 A6
Harbour Cres. CO12   17 H2
Harcourt Av. CO12   16 D3
Hazelville Clo. CO12   16 C6
Hewitt Rd. CO12   16 A6
High St. CO12   17 G3
Highfield Av. CO12   17 E4
Hill Rd. CO12   17 G3
Holyrood. CO12   16 C5
Hordle Pl. CO12   17 G3
Hordle St. CO12   17 G4
Howard Av. CO12   16 C5
Hudson Clo. CO12   16 D6
Ingestre St. CO12   17 G3
Jubilee Clo. CO12   16 C5
Keynes Way. CO12   16 D6
Kilmaine Rd. CO12   16 D5
King Georges Av. CO12   17 F4
Kings Clo. CO12   17 E4
Kings Head St. CO12   17 H1
Kings Quay St. CO12   17 H1
Kings Rd. CO12   17 E4
Kingsway. CO12   17 G3
Kreswell Gro. CO12   17 E5
Langley Clo. CO12   17 F4
Larksfield Cres. CO12   17 E3
Laurel Av. CO12   16 D5
Lee Rd. CO12   17 F4
Lime Av. CO12   17 E4
Litchfield. CO12   16 C5
Long Meadows. CO12   16 C5
Lourain Rd. CO12   17 E6
Low Rd, Dovercourt. CO12   17 E6
Low Rd,
  Upper Dovercourt. CO12   16 C6
Lower Marine Par. CO12   17 F5
Lynton Clo. CO12   17 E3
Main Rd. CO12   16 C5
Makins Rd. CO12   16 C2
Manor La. CO12   17 E4
Manor Rd. CO12   17 E4
Maple Clo. CO12   17 F4
Maria St. CO12   17 G2
Marine Par. CO12   17 G4
Market St. CO12   17 H1
Mayes La. CO12   16 A6
Mayflower Av. CO12   17 H2
Michaelstowe Dri. CO12   16 A5
Mill La. CO12   17 G4
Milton Rd. CO12   17 G3
Minerva Clo. CO12   16 D6
Nelson Rd. CO12   16 C6
Newport Clo. CO12   17 G3
Newton Rd. CO12   16 D4
Nightingale Clo. CO12   16 D6
Norway Cres. CO12   16 D4
Oakland Rd. CO12   17 F4
Oakley Rd. CO12   16 A6
Oakview. CO12   16 D6
Old Vicarage Rd. CO12   17 F4
Orwell Rd. CO12   17 G3
Oulton Clo. CO12   16 D4
Outpart Eastward. CO12   17 H1
Oxenford Clo. CO12   16 C6
Park Rd. CO12   17 F3
Parkeston Rd,
  Parkeston. CO12   16 D3
Parkeston Rd,
  Parkeston Quay. CO12   16 D2
Patricks La. CO12   17 F3
Pelham Clo. CO12   16 D5
Phoys St. CO12   17 G2
Portland Av. CO12   17 F4
Portland Cres. CO12   17 F4
Pound Farm Dri. CO12   16 D4
Princes Rd. CO12   17 E4
Princess St. CO12   16 D2
Promenade. CO12   17 F6
Queens Rd. CO12   17 E5
Ramsey Rd. CO12   16 A5
Ravden Clo. CO12   17 E3
Refinery Av. CO12   17 E4
Rehaven. CO12   16 A5
Rigbow Rd. CO12   16 D5
Refinery Rd. CO12   16 B2

Richmond Cres. CO12   17 E5
Rose Bank. CO12   16 D4
Rowan Clo. CO12   17 F4
Rowlands Yd. CO12   16 C5
St. Denis Clo. CO12   17 E6
St Edmunds Clo. CO12   17 E6
St Georges Av. CO12   17 F5
St Helens Grn. CO12   17 H2
St Michaels Rd. CO12   17 F5
Seafield Rd. CO12   17 F5
Second Av. CO12   17 F4
Shackleton Clo. CO12   16 D6
Shaftesbury Av. CO12   17 E3
Squat La. CO12   16 D5
Station La. CO12   17 F3
Station Rd,
  Dovercourt. CO12   17 G3
Station Rd,
  Harwich Grn. CO12   17 h2
Station Rd,
  Parkeston. CO12   16 C2
Stour Clo. CO12   16 A5
Stour Rd. CO12   17 G2
Sweden Clo. CO12   16 D4
Talbot St. CO12   17 G2
The Close. CO12   16 D4
The Dales. CO12   16 C6
The Drive. CO12   17 E5
The Green. CO12   16 C5
The Haven. CO12   16 D4
The Quay. CO12   17 G1
The Ridgeway. CO12   17 E4
The Vineway. CO12   17 E3
Third Av. CO12   17 F4
Tyler St. CO12   16 C2
Una Rd. CO12   16 C3
Valley Rd. CO12   16 B5
Vansittart St. CO12   17 G2
Vaux Av. CO12   16 C6
Victoria St. CO12   17 G3
Vienna Clo. CO12   17 E6
Waddesdon Rd. CO12   17 G3
Warham Rd. CO12   16 C5
Washington Rd. CO12   16 D5
Wellington Rd. CO12   17 H2
West Dock Rd. CO12   16 C2
West End La. CO12   17 E6
West St. CO12   17 G1
Whinfield Av. CO12   16 C6
Whitehart La. CO12   17 H1
Wick La. CO12   17 F3
William Grove Av. CO12   16 D5
Willoughby Rd. CO12   16 D5
Willow Way. CO12   16 D5
Witch Elm. CO12   16 C5

KELVEDON

Argyle Ct. CO5   26 B5
Avocet Clo. CO5   26 C6
Barnfield. CO5   26 C4
Bittern Clo. CO5   26 C5
Brockwell La. CO5   26 A6
Church Rd. CO5   26 B5
Church St. CO5   26 A5
Coggeshall Rd. CO5   26 B4
Croft Rd. CO5   26 A5
Curlew Clo. CO5   26 C6
Docwra Rd. CO5   26 B5
Dowches Dri. CO5   26 B5
Dowches Gdns. CO5   26 B5
Driffield Clo. CO5   26 C4
Dunlin Ct. CO5   26 C6
Easterford Rd. CO5   26 B6
Feering Hill. CO5   26 C5
Fullers Clo. CO5   26 A6
Gadwell Reach. CO5   26 C6
Glebe Rd. CO5   26 A5
*Godwit Ct,
  Widgeon Pl. CO5   26 B6
Greenways. CO5   26 B4
Greys Paddock. CO5   26 B6
Hall Farm Clo. CO5   26 D4
Harvest Ct. CO5   26 C5
Heron Rd. CO5   26 A6
High St. CO5   26 A6
Hunt Clo. CO5   26 D4
INDUSTRIAL ESTATES:
  Threshelfords
  Business Park. CO5   26 D5

Inworth Rd. CO5   26 D4
John Raven Ct. CO5   26 C5
Kelvedon By-Pass. CO5   26 D6
Kingfisher Way. CO5   26 C5
Lapwing Dri. CO5   26 B6
London Rd. CO5   26 D4
Maldon Rd. CO5   26 A6
Mallard Clo. CO5   26 C5
Marshall Clo. CO5   26 C4
Millers Mead. CO5   26 D4
New Rd. CO5   26 B5
Observer Way. CO5   26 B4
Orchard Rd. CO5   26 B5
Packe Clo. CO5   26 D4
Riverside Way. CO5   26 B6
Rolley La. CO5   26 B5
Rye Mill La. CO5   26 C6
St Marys Rd. CO5   26 B6
Sherwood Way. CO5   26 C4
Spa Rd. CO5   26 D4
Station Rd. CO5   26 C4
Swan St. CO5   26 C5
Teal Way. CO5   26 C6
Tern Clo. CO5   26 C5
The Chase. CO5   26 B6
Thorne Rd. CO5   26 A5
Threshelfords
  Business Park. CO5   26 D5
Trews Gdns. CO5   26 B5
Wagtail Pl. CO5   26 B6
Watermill Rd. CO5   26 D4
Widgeon Pl. CO5   26 B6
Worlds End La. CO5   26 C5

MANNINGTREE

Alma Sq. CO11   27 B1
Barnfield. CO11   27 A2
Beckford Rd. CO11   27 D2
Bendalls Ct. CO11   27 A1
Brook St. CO11   27 A1
Brunswick Ho Cut. CO11   27 D2
California Rd. CO11   27 D2
Cambria Clo. CO11   27 D2
Cedar Cres. CO11   27 A2
Chapel Cut. CO11   27 D2
Church La. CO11   27 C2
Colchester Rd. CO11   27 A2
College Ct. CO11   27 A1
Elmdale Dri. CO11   27 A2
Falklands Rd. CO11   27 B2
Gas Field. CO11   27 B1
Green La. CO11   27 C2
Harwich Rd. CO11   27 D2
High St,
  Manningtree. CO11   27 A1
High St, Mistley. CO11   27 C1
Hilton Clo. CO11   27 B1
Horsleycross Rd. CO11   27 A3
Kerridges Cut. CO11   27 D2
Long Rd. CO11   27 A3
Lushington Rd. CO11   27 A1
Malthouse Rd. CO11   27 B1
Middlefield Rd. CO11   27 D2
Mill La. CO11   27 A2
New Rd. CO11   27 A2
Norman Rd. CO11   27 B2
North St. CO11   27 A1
Oxford Rd. CO11   27 A2
Quay St. CO11   27 A1
Queensway. CO11   27 A1
Railway St. CO11   27 A2
Regent St. CO11   27 A1
Remercie Rd. CO11   27 D2
Rigby Av. CO11   27 D2
Rigby Rd. CO11   27 D2
Riverside Av E. CO11   27 A1
Riverside Av W. CO11   27 A1
Riverview Vs. CO11   27 A2
St Michaels St. CO11   27 A1
School La. CO11   27 C2
Seafield Av. CO11   27 D2
Shrubland Rd. CO11   27 D2
South St. CO11   27 A2
Station Rd. CO11   27 A1
Stour St. CO11   27 A1
Stour View Av. CO11   27 D2
Stour View Clo. CO11   27 D2
Swan Ct. CO11   27 D2

The Green. CO11   27 C1
The Lane. CO11   27 C1
The Park. CO11   27 B2
The Walls. CO11   27 B1
Trinity Clo. CO11   27 A2
Trinity Rd. CO11   27 A2
Victoria Cres. CO11   27 A1
Westmorland Clo. CO11   27 D2
York St. CO11   27 A2

WALTON/ FRINTON

Addison Rd. CO13   22 A4
Agar Rd. CO14   23 H2
Agar Road App. CO14   23 H2
Alfred Ter. CO14   23 H1
Ashes Clo. CO14   23 E1
Ashlyns Rd. CO13   22 D5
Ashmole Dri. CO13   23 E3
Audley Way. CO13   23 F3
Audries Est. CO14   23 E1
Avocet Clo. CO13   22 D3
Bardfield Way. CO13   23 E3
Baynards Cres. CO13   22 D3
Beaumont Clo. CO14   23 E2
Beechcroft Av. CO13   22 C3
Bellamy Clo. CO13   22 C3
Bemerton Gdns. CO13   22 B3
Bennett Clo. CO14   23 F1
Bernards Clo. CO13   22 D3
Beverley Dri. CO13   22 D2
Blaine Dri. CO13   22 D3
Blanchard Clo. CO13   22 A3
Bloomfield Av. CO13   22 D2
Brambles. CO14   23 F2
Branscombe Clo. CO13   22 D4
Brent Clo. CO13   22 D3
Brian Bishop Clo. CO14   23 G1
Briarfields. CO13   22 B1
Brightside. CO13   22 D2
Bruff Clo. CO14   23 F2
Buckfast Av. CO13   22 C3
Burnham Clo. CO14   23 F2
Bushell Way. CO13   22 D4
Butchers La. CO14   23 G2
Cambridge Rd. CO13   23 F4
Capel Park. CO13   22 B1
Cedar Clo. CO14   23 F3
Central Av. CO13   23 F3
Chamberlain Av. CO14   23 G2
Chapel Fields. CO13   22 D4
Chaplins. CO13   23 E3
Charlotte Dri. CO13   22 D3
Charnock Clo. CO13   23 E3
Chartfield Dri. CO13   22 C1
Chelmer Dri. CO13   22 D3
Chestnut Av. CO13   22 B3
Church La. CO13   22 A6
Church Rd. CO13   23 H1
Churchfield Rd. CO14   23 H1
Claire Rd. CO13   22 A3
Clays Rd. CO14   23 F2
Cliff Way. CO13   23 F4
Coles La. CO14   23 F1
Columbine Gdns. CO14   23 F3
Connaught Av. CO13   23 E4
Corton Croft Clo. CO13   23 E2
Crabtree Clo. CO13   22 B1
Cranford Clo. CO13   22 D4
Crescent Rd. CO14   23 H2
Crossfields Way. CO13   22 B3
D'Arcy Rd. CO13   23 E3
Dead La. CO13   22 B4
Deveraux Clo. CO14   23 E2
Dugmore Av. CO13   22 B1
Eagle Av. CO14   23 H1
Easton Way. CO13   23 G3
Edenside. CO13   23 E2
Edith Av. CO13   22 C1
Elliots Dri. CO14   23 G1
Elm Gro. CO13   22 C3
Elm Tree Av. CO13   23 E1
Elm Tree Clo. CO13   23 E3
Esplanade. CO13   23 E6
Eton Rd. CO13   23 F4
Ferndown Rd. CO13   22 D4
Field Walk. CO14   23 F2
Fifth Av. CO13   22 D4

First Av. CO13	22 D5
Five Acres. CO14	23 G1
Fourth Av. CO13	23 E5
Frietuna Rd. CO13	22 D3
Frinton Rd. CO13	22 B3
Garden Rd. CO14	23 E2
Gatefield Clo. CO14	23 E2
Gatefield Ct. CO14	23 E2
Glebe Way. CO13	23 E4
Gouldings Av. CO14	23 G1
Graces Walk. CO13	23 F4
Grange Clo. CO14	23 F2
Grasmere Gdns. CO13	23 E2
Grass Field. CO13	22 D3
Great Harrods. CO14	23 F2
Green End La. CO13	22 A5
Green Rd. CO13	23 E4
Grimston Way. CO14	23 G2
Grove Av. CO14	23 G1
Hadleigh Rd. CO13	23 E5
Halstead Rd. CO13	22 B3
Hanover Ct. CO14	23 F1
Harold Gro. CO13	23 E5
Harold Rd. CO13	23 E5
Harold Way. CO13	23 E5
Haslemere Gdns. CO13	23 E2
Hawthorns. CO13	23 E2
Heron Way. CO13	22 D3
Heronsgate. CO13	23 E3
Hervilly Way. CO14	23 G2
High St. CO14	23 H1
Hill Crest. CO13	22 C1
Hillside. CO13	22 D5
Hogarth End. CO13	22 D2
Holland Rd, Frinton-on-Sea. CO13	22 D6
Holland Rd, Kirby Cross. CO13	22 B3
Holledge Cres. CO13	22 D5
Holmbrook Way. CO13	22 D5
Honywood Way. CO13	23 E2
Hopkins Clo. CO13	23 E3
Horsey Rd. CO13	22 B1
Hubbards Chase. CO14	23 G1
Huntway. CO13	22 D3
Island La. CO13	22 D1
Jubilee Way. CO13	23 E3
Keswick Clo. CO13	23 E2
Kino Rd. CO14	23 H1
Kirby Rd. CO13	22 A5
Kirby Rd. CO14	23 E1
Kirkbaye. CO13	22 D3
Laburnum Cres. CO13	22 C3
Laxton Gro. CO13	22 A5
Little Baker. CO14	23 F2
Little Harrods. CO14	23 F2
Little Wood. CO13	22 D3
Long La. CO13	22 B6
Lowe Chase. CO14	23 G1
Luff Way. CO14	23 E2
Lumber Leys. CO14	23 F2
Lushington Av. CO13	22 D4
Lynne Clo. CO13	22 D3
Main Rd. CO13	22 A6
Mandeville Way. CO13	23 E3
Manor Rd. CO13	22 A6
Maple Dri. CO13	22 C3
Marina Mews. CO14	23 H1
Marney Way. CO13	23 G3
Martello Cres. CO14	23 H1
Meadowcroft Clo. CO13	23 E3
Mill La. CO13	23 H1
Modlen Rd. CO14	23 F2
Mumfords La. CO13	22 A2
New Pier St. CO14	23 H2
Newgate St. CO14	23 H1

Newport Way. CO13	23 F3
North St. CO14	23 H1
Norwood Way. CO14	23 F2
Oakwood Clo. CO13	22 D4
Ockendon Way. CO14	23 F2
Old Parsonage Way. CO13	23 E4
Old Pier St. CO14	23 H1
Old Rd. CO13	23 E5
Old Way. CO13	23 E5
Orchard Dri. CO13	22 A5
Oxford Rd. CO13	23 F4
Paternoster Row. CO14	23 H1
Peacehaven. CO13	23 F4
Percival Rd. CO13	22 C1
Philip Clo. CO14	23 F2
Pightle Way. CO14	23 F2
Pine Wood Clo. CO13	22 C4
Plover Clo. CO13	22 D3
Pointer Pl. CO13	22 D2
Pole Barn La. CO13	23 E4
Polley Clo. CO13	22 D2
Poplar Way. CO13	22 C3
Portobello Rd. CO14	23 H1
Prospect Park. CO13	22 A4
Pulpitfield Clo. CO14	23 F2
Pyesand. CO13	22 B1
Quay La. CO13	22 C1
Queens Rd. CO13	23 E5
Quendon Way. CO13	23 F4
Raeburn Clo. CO13	23 E2
Raglan Rd. CO13	23 E5
Rainham Way. CO13	23 F3
Rectory Rd. CO13	22 A6
Reynards Clo. CO13	22 D3
Rigdons La. CO14	23 F1
Rochford Way. CO14	23 E2
Rokell Way. CO13	23 E3
Romney Clo. CO13	22 D2
Roydon Way. CO13	23 E3
Sadlers Clo. CO13	22 C3
St Botolphs Ter. CO14	23 G2
St Marys Rd. CO13	23 E4
Saville St. CO14	23 H1
School Rd. CO13	22 D4
Seaview Heights. CO14	23 G2
Second Av. CO13	22 D5
Shaw Clo. CO13	23 E3
Sherborne Clo. CO13	23 E2
Short La. CO13	22 B6
Skyrmans Fee. CO13	22 D3
Slaters Clo. CO13	22 D3
South Croft Clo. CO13	22 B3
Southcliff Par. CO14	23 H2
Southcliff Prom. CO14	23 G3
Southview Dri. CO13	23 G2
Snape Clo. CO13	22 D3
Stablefields Rd. CO14	23 F2
Stafford Clo. CO13	22 D3
Stallards Cres. CO13	22 D4
Standley Rd. CO14	23 H1
Stansted Way. CO13	23 F3
Station Rd. CO13	22 A3
Station St. CO14	23 H2
Stewards Clo. CO13	23 E3
Stratford Pl. CO14	23 H1
Stubbs Clo. CO13	22 D3
Suffolk St. CO14	23 H1
Sunningdale Way. CO13	22 D2
Sycamore Way. CO13	22 C3
Temple Clo. CO13	23 F3
The Birches. CO13	22 D3
The Close, Frinton. CO13	22 D4
The Close, Gt Holland. CO13	22 A6
The Crescent. CO13	23 E5
The Larneys. CO13	22 D2

The Leas. CO13	23 F3
The Linnets. CO13	22 A3
The Meers. CO13	22 D3
The Mews. CO13	23 F4
The Oaks. CO13	23 E4
The Parade. CO14	23 H2
The Path Way. CO13	22 D3
The Ridge. CO14	23 F1
The Sparlings. CO13	22 B1
The Stokes. CO14	23 G1
The Street. CO13	22 B1
The Warrens. CO13	22 D3
Third Av. CO13	22 D5
Thornhill Clo. CO13	23 E2
Thorns Way. CO14	23 F2
Thorpe Rd. CO13	22 A3
Turpins La. CO13	22 D3
Upper Fourth Av. CO13	23 E4
Upper Second Av. CO13	22 D4
Upper Third Av. CO13	22 D4
Valley Walk. CO14	23 G2
Vicarage La. CO14	23 H1
Victoria Av. CO13	22 C1
Victoria Rd. CO13	23 G1
Village Clo. CO13	22 C3
Village Way. CO13	22 C3
Vista Av. CO13	22 C1
Wade Reach. CO14	23 F1
Walden Way. CO13	23 E4
Waltham Way. CO13	23 F4
Walton Rd. CO13	22 D1
Warde Chase. CO14	23 G1
Warley Way. CO13	23 G3
Wavring Av. CO13	22 D3
Wellfield Way. CO13	22 D3
West St. CO13	23 H1
Westbury Rd. CO13	22 A5
Willow Av. CO13	22 C3
Wimborne Clo. CO13	23 E3
Winchester Rd. CO13	23 F4
Winterbournes. CO14	23 F2
Witton Wood. CO13	22 D4
Witton Wood La. CO13	22 D4
Woburn Av. CO13	22 C3
Woodberry Way. CO13	23 G3
Woodfield Clo. CO14	23 F2
Woodside. CO14	23 F3

WEST MERSEA

Alexandra Av. CO5	27 D4
Avocet Clo. CO5	27 C5
Barfield Rd. CO5	27 B5
Beach Rd. CO5	27 B6
Beverley Av. CO5	27 D5
Birchwood Clo. CO5	27 D5
Blackwater Clo. CO5	27 A5
Brambledown. CO5	27 C5
Brickhouse Clo. CO5	27 B4
Brierley Av. CO5	27 D4
Broomhills Av. CO5	27 C6
Buxey Clo. CO5	27 B5
Captains Rd. CO5	27 B6
Carrington Ct. CO5	27 C4
*Chandlers Clo, Upland Cres. CO5	27 C5
Chandlers Ct. CO5	27 B5
Chatsworth Rd. CO5	27 C4
Church Rd. CO5	27 B6
Churchfields. CO5	27 B6
City Rd. CO5	27 A5
Coast Rd. CO5	27 A5
Colchester Rd. CO5	27 C4
Cypress Mews. CO5	27 B5

East Rd. CO5	27
Elmwood Dri. CO5	27
Empress Av. CO5	27
Empress Dri. CO5	27
Fairhaven Av. CO5	27
Firs Chase. CO5	27
Firs Hamlet. CO5	27
Firs Rd. CO5	27
Gainsborough Clo. CO5	27
Garden Farm. CO5	27
Goings La. CO5	27
Grays Clo. CO5	27
Grove Av. CO5	27
Gunfleet Clo. CO5	27
High St. CO5	27
High St Nth. CO5	27
Hogarth Clo. CO5	27
King Charles Rd. CO5	27
Kingsland Beach. CO5	27
Kingsland Rd. CO5	27
Kingsmere Clo. CO5	27
Langwood. CO5	27
Lawns Clo. CO5	27
Lea Side. CO5	27
Meadow La. CO5	27
Melrose Rd. CO5	27
Mersea Av. CO5	27
Mill Rd. CO5	27
New Captains Rd. CO5	27
Norfolk Av. CO5	27
Oakwood Av. CO5	27
Oakwood Dri. CO5	27
Oakwood Gdns. CO5	27
Oyster Clo. CO5	27
Pine Gro. CO5	27
Pyefleet House. CO5	27
Queen Anne Dri. CO5	27
Queen Anne Gdns. CO5	27
Queen Anne Rd. CO5	27
Queensbury Clo. CO5	27
Rainbow Rd. CO5	27
Ray House. CO5	27
Reymead Clo. CO5	27
Richmond Rd. CO5	27
Rosebank Rd. CO5	27
Rushmere Clo. CO5	27
St Peters Rd. CO5	27
Sea View Av. CO5	27
Shears Cres. CO5	27
Spruce Clo. CO5	27
Stable Clo. CO5	27
Stonehill Way. CO5	27
Strood Clo. CO5	27
Suffolk Av. CO5	27
The Coverts. CO5	27
The Lane. CO5	27
The Orchard. CO5	27
The Paddock. CO5	27
Thornwood Clo. CO5	27
Trinity Clo. CO5	27
Trinity Mews. CO5	27
Upland Cres. CO5	27
Upland Rd. CO5	27
Victoria Esplanade. CO5	27
Victory Rd. CO5	27
Vince Clo. CO5	27
Whittaker Way. CO5	27
Willoughby Av. CO5	27
Windsor House. CO5	27
Windsor Rd. CO5	27
Woodfield Dri. CO5	27
Woodstock. CO5	27
Yorick Av. CO5	27
Yorick Rd. CO5	27